7/89

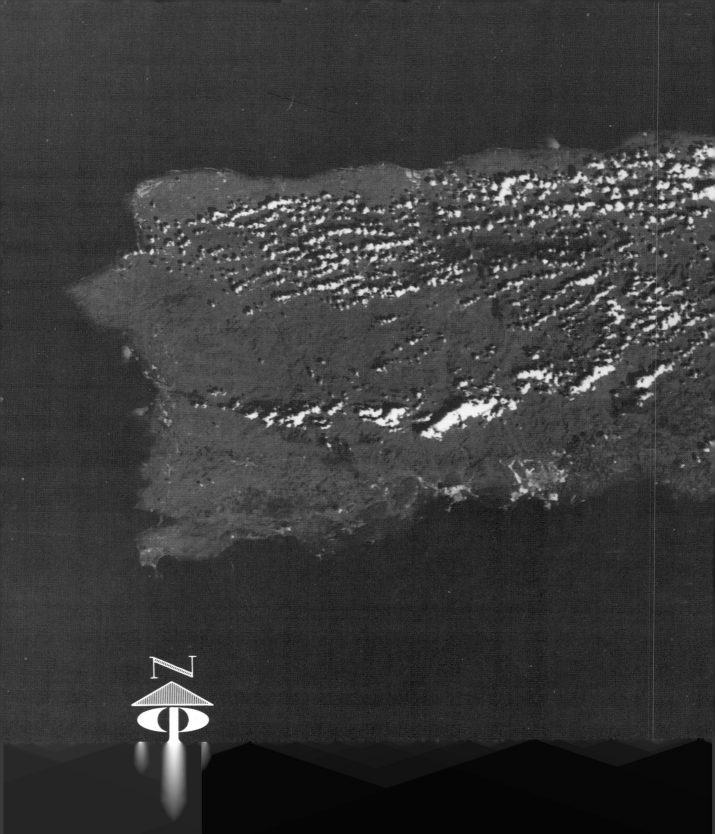

The New
Enchantment of America

FAR-FLUNG
AMERICA

By Allan Carpenter

 CHILDREN'S PRESS CHICAGO

ACKNOWLEDGMENTS

For assistance in the preparation of the revised edition, the author thanks:
Consultant ODESSA M. MITCHELL, Office Manager, Territorial Affairs, United States Department of the Interior; Tourism Development Company, Commonwealth of Puerto Rico; ERWIN D. CANHAM, Resident Commissioner, Government of the Northern Mariana Islands; and Photojournalism and Public Inquiries Branch, Department of the Navy, U.S.A.

American Airlines—Anne Vitaliano, Director of Public Relations; *Capitol Historical Society*, Washington, D. C.; *Newberry Library*, Chicago, Dr. Lawrence Towner, Director; *Northwestern University Library*, Evanston, Illinois; *United Airlines*—John P. Grember, Manager of Special Promotions; Joseph P. Hopkins, Manager, News Bureau; Carl Provorse, *Carpenter Publishing House.*

UNITED STATES GOVERNMENT AGENCIES: *Department of Agriculture*—Robert Hailstock, Jr., Photography Division, Office of Communication; Donald C. Schuhart, Information Division, Soil Conservation Service. *Army*—Doran Topolosky, Public Affairs Office, Chief of Engineers, Corps of Engineers. *Department of Interior*—Louis Churchville, Director of Communications; EROS Space Program—Phillis Wiepking, Community Affairs; Charles Withington, Geologist; Mrs. Ruth Herbert, Information Specialist; Bureau of Reclamation; National Park Service—Fred Bell and the individual sites; Fish and Wildlife Service—Bob Hinne, Public Affairs Office. *Library of Congress*—Dr. Alan Fern, Director of the Department of Research; Sara Wallace, Director of Publications; Dr. Walter W. Ristow, Chief, Geography and Map Division; Herbert Sandborn, Exhibits Officer. *National Archives*—Dr. James B. Rhoads, Archivist of the United States; Albert Meisel, Assistant Archivist for Educational Programs; David Eggenberger, Publications Director; Bill Leary, Still Picture Reference; James Moore, Audio-Visual Archives. *United States Postal Service*—Herb Harris, Stamps Division.

For assistance in the preparation of the first edition, the author thanks:
Consultants Ruth G. Van Cleve, Director, Office of Territories, U.S. Department of Interior; G. Etzel Pearcy, Geographer, Bureau of Intelligence and Research, U.S. Department of State; and Danilo Ondina, Director, Commonwealth of Puerto Rico, Economic Development Administration, Continental Operations Branch; and Dean Rusk, Secretary of State; Robert S. McNamara, Secretary of Defense; Stewart L. Udall, Secretary of the Interior, Robert Sanchez Vilella, Governor, Commonwealth of Puerto Rico; Ralph M. Paiewonsky, Governor, The Virgin Islands; Manuel F.L. Guerrero, Governor, Guam; H. Rex Lee, Governor, American Samoa; Robert J. Fleming, Jr., Governor, Panama Canal Zone; and M.W. Goding, High Commissioner, Trust Territory of the Pacific Islands.

Illustrations on the preceding pages:
Cover photograph: Guam, Pacific Area Travel Association
Page 1: Commemorative stamps of historic interest
Pages 2-3: Trunk Bay, St. John, Virgin Islands, USDI, National Park Service, Virgin Islands National Park
Pages 4-5: Puerto Rico, General Electric

Project Editor, Revised Edition:
 Joan Downing
Assistant Editor, Revised Edition:
 Mary Reidy
Library of Congress Cataloging in Publication Data
Carpenter, John Allan, 1917-
 Far-flung America.
 (His The new enchantment of America)
 Includes index.
 1. United States—Insular possessions—Juvenile literature.   2.   Canal Zone—Juvenile literature.   I.   Title.
 II.   Series.
 F970.C35   1979   970   79-12505
 ISBN 0-516-04152-5

Contents

The flags of American Samoa and United States in Pago Pago.

Setting the Scene

Somewhere, half a world away, American children are studying English under the most modern system of television instruction anywhere—in a land where the American flag flies below the equator—where there is winter during the North American summer—where the legislature meets with its members wearing their native garments, the lavalava—where thatched huts still prevail.

In another equally faraway spot, Old Glory waves from the top of what would be the highest mountain in the world if most of it were not underwater—where one of the favorite sports is racing the lumbering pink-tongued water buffalo or carabao—where skeletons have been found of what may have been a race of giants—where the loyal natives are proud to be American citizens.

The Stars and Stripes are hoisted every morning in a land where once stood the greatest fortresses of the Spanish empire—where tiny orchids no larger than the heads of pins bloom—where nature's nightly serenades are not by birds but by lyrical frogs with flute-like voices—where the American citizens have recently accomplished such remarkable achievements that people from all over the world have come to study them.

In the midst of the lonely Pacific the Star-Spangled Banner soars above territory where the greatest problem is a huge, friendly, clumsy bird.

America has interests in another region so vast that its tiny parts are spread over an area as large as the entire mainland United States and yet there is not enough land area to cover more than half of Long Island.

One of our most important interests is a great transportation system that carries ships *eastward* from the Atlantic to the Pacific. America holds sway in lands of perpetual spring where the climate is so good it can be guaranteed, and in other lands where oppressive tropical heat clings almost perpetually.

All of these facts are only a tantalizing hint of the vast extent and variety of territories of the United States and regions under United States control.

Few mainlanders realize how far away the flag has taken their fellow countrymen. Probably fewer still consider the fact that loyal and patriotic American citizens and American nationals are natives of American lands stretched from the eastern Caribbean to the south seas, and almost to the Orient.

The histories, problems, resources, hopes, and joys of these people and their lands are truly the stories of America and Americans, no matter how remote or how unusual they may seem to other Americans on the mainland.

This book attempts to reveal something about these lands and their peoples as another of the wonderful stories of the enchantment of America.

Below: A panorama of Puerto Rico.
Opposite: Coca Falls, Puerto Rico.

AMERICA
IN THE
CARIBBEAN

Figure 1

OUTLYING AREAS OF THE UNITED STATES IN THE CARIBBEAN

Courtesy Bureau of Intelligence and Research, Office of the Geographer, United States Department of State

Puerto Rico

LAY OF THE LAND

Those who love Puerto Rico are apt to say, "It is as close to paradise as man will ever see." This "paradise" is a comparatively small island, about 100 miles (161 kilometers) long and 36 miles (58 kilometers) wide. Waves of the Atlantic lap on the gleaming beaches of the northern part, and the blue Caribbean splashes on the southern shores. It is classified as the smallest of the Caribbean island group known as the Greater Antilles.

The nearest neighbors of Puerto Rico are the Virgin Islands, just 34 miles (55 kilometers) to the east. The Dominican Republic on the island of Hispaniola lies slightly more than 70 miles (113 kilometers) to the west. The channels between Puerto Rico and its neighbors are among the most important sea entrances to the Caribbean on the route from Europe to the Panama Canal. The nearest point of the United States mainland is 885 miles (1,424 kilometers) away.

The largest of Puerto Rico's offshore islands are Vieques, 51 square miles (132 square kilometers), lying 9 miles (14 kilometers) east of Puerto Rico; Culebra, 11 square miles (28 square kilometers), 18 miles (29 kilometers) to the east, with its splendid harbor of Puerto Grande; and Mona, 20 square miles (52 square kilometers), 40 miles (64 kilometers) off the west coast. Near these smaller islands are still smaller islands, such as Culebrita off Culebra.

Those not familiar with Puerto Rico are surprised that much of the interior is mountainous. The peaks run roughly from east to west, and lowlands lie across the north and south coasts. The highest point in Puerto Rico is 4,389 feet (1,338 meters), but there is no continuous high ridge that prevents roads from crossing the island at a number of points. The northern section, even in the area close to the sea, is dotted with low hills, breaking up the level ground. Strange "haystack" formations are among the hills found in northern Puerto Rico. They are the remains of limestone caves that collapsed and left rough ground. A large part of the flat coastal land is found in the

The coast of San Juan.

south. Most rugged of the Puerto Rican mountains is hulking El Yunque (The Anvil), 3,494 feet (1,065 meters) high, the towering landmark of the northeast.

Rivers course down from the mountains to all coasts of the island. The principal river of Puerto Rico is La Plata, emptying into the Atlantic west of San Juan. Other northern rivers are Loíza, Cibuco, Manatí, Arecibo, and Guajataca. Rivers flowing to the west are Culebrinas, Añasco and Guanajibo; southern streams are Yauco, Tallaboa, Jacaquas, Coamo, and Patillas. To the east flow the Guaynés, Blanco, and Fajardo rivers. The rivers are generally useless for transportation, but have great potential for hydroelectric development.

The principal lakes are Carite, Patillas, Guayabal, Guajataca; in addition are Caonillas, Loíza, and Yauco reservoirs.

Puerto Rico is a "land where temperatures are spring-like the year around." Temperatures average only six degrees apart between winter and summer, and in the mountains, temperatures are five to ten degrees cooler. Where the northeast trade winds blow, the heat is never intense, and it is always comfortable in the shade. The nights are cool, and this is said to be why the people of Puerto Rico are so vigorous as compared to those of other lands of continuing warmth.

One hundred eighty inches (4.6 meters) of rain falls on El Yunque every year, giving it a "rain forest" climate. In the island's opposite corner, the Lajas Valley of the southwest is so dry as to be almost

El Yunque rain forest

desert-like. Because of the warm winds, the ground dries out quickly, and, almost anywhere on the island, if two weeks go by without rain, it becomes a drought period.

The major weather problem of Puerto Rico is the hurricane. The first one of these mighty blows recorded was in 1515. In 1526 an observer wrote, "There was a great deal of wind and rain which lasted twenty-four hours. . . . The damage caused by the flooding of the plantations is greater than one can estimate. Many rich men have grown poor." Almost the same conditions prevail today when one of these infrequent but devastating storms arrives.

The natives said that such storms were caused by the evil god Juracán, whose name was changed so that these storms became known as "hurricanes." In Puerto Rico, hurricanes are not given women's names. For some reason they are named for the saints' days on which they fall.

FOOTSTEPS ON THE LAND

Not much is known about an ancient cave-dwelling people who some think once lived in Puerto Rico and who may have left picture writings called pictographs and other articles in caves of the islands. At a much later time a group of natives began moving up from South America across the string of islands called the Lesser Antilles. Finally they reached Puerto Rico and then the northern and westernmost of the larger islands of the Greater Antilles were at last occupied by them. These people were known as the Arawak.

In a still later period a group of fierce, warlike people called Caribs also migrated from South America and began to occupy the Lesser Antilles, one by one. By the time Europeans reached the Caribbean, the dreaded Caribs had arrived at the outskirts of Puerto Rico and had occupied the offshore islands of Vieques and Culebra. They made murderous raids on the peaceful Arawak inhabitants of Puerto Rico, often carrying captives off into slavery.

The *Borinqueño,* as the native people of Puerto Rico were called, took the worst of the Caribs attacks, and Borinquen (the native

16

name for Puerto Rico) became a sort of shield for the other islands of the Greater Antilles against the Caribs. So much feared and respected were the awful Caribs that they gave their name to the whole region—the Caribbean.

Native Borinquen towns such as Coamo and Caguas had apparently been inhabited for hundreds of years. Their simple houses, called bohío, were mere grass huts set up on stilts. They were mostly an agricultural people, raising maize, yams, squash, potatoes, and various tropical fruits such as citron. They may have domesticated over two hundred food plants. The *Borinqueño* girdled trees and set large areas on fire to clear the land. Ashes from the flames helped overcome the acidity of the tropical soil and make better crops. Probably most of the island had been burned over in this way any number of times.

Although they were not primarily hunters, the Arawak natives roasted iguana lizards, rodents, and larvae of insects for food. The enormous piles of shells they left behind show how fond they were of shellfish. Fish and turtles were popular food, and even the plump, tough dugong may have been eaten occasionally.

Only the women wore any clothing—a small apron. The *Borin-queño* knew how to make a carved reclining chair called a *duho,* and they slept and generally died in simple hammocks. They produced crude painted earthen pottery, carved some stone jewelry, and made ceremonial masks.

The skill of the Carib people was mostly shown in their *pirogues,* cleverly and patiently hollowed out of huge logs. In these the plundering cannibals scoured the seas.

"¡QUE RICO PUERTO!"

Christopher Columbus discovered Borinquen on his second voyage to the New World in 1493. According to Columbus' son, Diego, the admiral sent men ashore on November 16 and found a neat Indian village, laid out around a "plaza." Just where this first landing was made is still disputed.

Famous Spanish explorer and colonizer Don Juan Ponce de León brought fifty men to Borinquen in 1508 to make the first Spanish settlement. The legend is told that when Ponce saw the beautiful harbor of San Juan he exclaimed *"Que rico puerto"* (what a rich port), giving Puerto Rico its future name. The natives considered the Spanish to be superior beings—bearded white immortals—and treated them with great respect.

They gave Ponce some yellow discs that he admired. When these turned out to be pure gold, Ponce put the natives to work finding the yellow specks in the sand. They soon tired of this unaccustomed work. A chief gave orders to test the divinity of these strangers. His followers drowned a young Spaniard in a stream and waited for three days to see if he would perform a supernatural act. When the decaying body indicated that Spaniards were mortals, the natives revolted.

The rebellion was soon smashed, as were others that followed. The natives were at last enslaved and for the next three hundred years the island formed the key outpost of the Spanish empire in the New World—known as "San Juan Bautista de Puerto Rico," or Puerto Rico for short. The town that had been known first as Caparra, then Puerto Rico, was later called San Juan. As early as 1511 Puerto Rico was granted its own official seal, the first of any Spanish colony in the New World.

Under awful conditions of forced labor, the native population declined with unbelievable speed from an estimated thirty thousand when the island was first discovered to a mere handful in less than fifty years. To make up this loss many upper-class Spaniards, mostly from the Province of Andalucia, migrated to Puerto Rico. They were a hardy group. "Had they not been," according to one writer, "Puerto Rico could hardly have survived. The tenacity of the settlers is one of the remarkable feats in the early colonial history of the New World."

GIBRALTAR OF THE NEW WORLD

The fortress of El Morro, second strongest in Spain's New World

El Morro Fortress was used to protect the Bay of San Juan.

empire, was completed in 1595, and not a moment too soon. English freebooter Sir Francis Drake attacked the port of San Juan. He was defeated, and it is recorded that one of the guns from El Morro "stroke the stoole from under him." In 1598 San Juan was captured by the Earl of Cumberland who was determined to "possesse the keyes of all the Indies" for Queen Elizabeth I of England. He could not hold out for long, and soon loaded his ships with all the hides, ginger, and sugar he could find and sailed away.

French, Dutch, and English corsairs attacked off and on over the decades. Privateers and pirates also plagued the island. Miguel Henriquez, one of the most successful of the privateers, scoured the Caribbean for thirty years. Spain tried to keep the commerce of Puerto Rico to herself, but smuggling was carried on everywhere. In

One of six gates in the old city wall of San Juan.

spite of all this, Puerto Rico remained a loyal, though not very prosperous, part of the Spanish dominions.

In 1797 El Morro's mighty fortress partner, San Cristobal, had just been completed when an English force of ten thousand men under Sir Ralph Abercromby failed in an attempt to capture San Juan. "Whoever has viewed the fortifications of Puerto Rico," one analyst wrote later, "must feel surprised that . . . a force of scarcely 10,000 men should lay siege to this place." Another writer notes, "One may still experience this sense of surprise—the fortifications are still there."

Large numbers of Spanish loyalists migrated to Puerto Rico in the late 1700s and early 1800s. A successful drive in 1815 was aimed at promoting the population, commerce, and agriculture of the island. Over the years the loyalty of the island to Spain was unusual and outstanding. Only one small revolutionary movement ever was tried; this, in 1868, soon fizzled out. Slavery was gradually and peacefully abolished by 1873 at the request of the people themselves.

At last in 1898 Spain granted to Puerto Rico *La Carta autonómica,* which made the island a dominion, with the right to settle its local affairs at home. Then the United States went to war with Spain in that year. American Admiral William Sampson bombarded San Juan, and the first American troops, under General Nelson A. Miles, landed at Guanica. Spain soon ceded Puerto Rico to the United States. The newly granted dominion status was discarded. Many Puerto Ricans felt that the work of almost four hundred years was blown away almost overnight.

YESTERDAY AND TODAY

The years that followed were ones of long and sometimes painful adjustment on both sides. The Foraker Act that established a civil government in Puerto Rico did not make Puerto Ricans United States citizens. The island was considered a U.S. possession.

President Theodore Roosevelt constantly prodded Congress to give Puerto Ricans citizenship, and Secretary of War Henry L. Stimson was also a great friend of Puerto Rico in America. In 1917 the Jones Act, sponsored by Congressman William A. Jones of Virginia and Horace M. Towner of Iowa, finally granted Puerto Ricans United States citizenship.

Most people thought that if the situation were to be further improved, Puerto Rico would either have to become a state of the United States or to become completely independent. However, such men as Stimson, Congressman Towner, and Puerto Rican governor in 1929, Theodore Roosevelt, Jr., predicted that an alternative to these forms could be found—possibly something like the old Spanish Dominion status granted in 1898.

The population of Puerto Rico had increased to a million and a half and very little had been done to improve the worsening condition of the people. Governor Roosevelt called them the "Children of Famine." He wrote, "Riding through the hills, I have stopped at farm after farm where lean, underfed women and sickly men repeated again and again the same story—little food and no opportunity to get more. From these hills the people have streamed into the coastal towns, increasing the already severe unemployment situation there. . . ." Sugar and coffee production and profits had grown tremendously, but the people had little chance to share in their success.

"In 1940," Jorge Felices-Pietrantoni writes, "the people of Puerto Rico resolved that poverty was intolerable even in a densely-populated country with too little land for agriculture and practically no natural resources for manufacturing."

The economic development program they devised to overcome all that is known popularly as "Operation Bootstrap." It brought the people "from a spirit of hopelessness to one of self-help and determination." Operation Bootstrap became one of the world's best-known efforts to improve the lot of mankind.

THE GOVERNMENT

Meanwhile the varying points of view regarding the political status

City Hall in San Juan. The present clock was installed in 1889.

of Puerto Rico continued to be discussed. It became clear that Puerto Ricans needed control over their own affairs and responsibility for solving their own problems. However, it was clear also that continued association with the United States was desired.

In 1947 the Jones Act was amended so that the governor could be chosen by the people, and in 1949 popular Luis Muñoz Marin became the first popularly elected governor. In 1950 Congress approved a law permitting the people of Puerto Rico to select their own government. Two years later they adopted a constitution that was ratified by Congress, and on July 25, 1952, the Commonwealth of Puerto Rico was proclaimed—to be known as *Estado Libre Asociado*—"Associated Free State."

Puerto Rico has become a self-governing community of United States citizens associated with the federal government by compact and mutual consent. Former Chief Justice Earl Warren said, "The new institution of the Commonwealth of Puerto Rico represents an experiment—the newest experiment and perhaps the most notable of American governmental experiments in our lifetime."

The commonwealth has a voice in Congress through a resident commissioner, elected by the people for a four-year term. He sits in the House of Representatives at Washington with all the privileges of a member of Congress except voting. Puerto Ricans do not have a vote in national elections of the United States, and consequently, in line with the principal of no taxation without representation, federal taxes for the most part are not applied to them. The United States Constitution remains the supreme law of Puerto Rico, and its highest court is the Supreme Court of the United States. Puerto Rico also enjoys free trade with the United States.

The constitution of Puerto Rico has spelled out a number of human rights and freedoms more clearly than the United States Constitution. Lawmaking is carried out by the Legislative Assembly, consisting of the Senate and the House of Representatives, with members elected by direct vote at each general election. The governor is elected for a term of four years.

The people of Puerto Rico can amend their own constitution. They can also call for changes in the relationship of Puerto Rico with the United States as governed by the Federal Relations Act. The Statehood Republican Party, advocating that Puerto Rico should become a full state of the United States, received better than a third of the vote in the 1964 elections. The *Partido Pro Independencia,* which favors an independent republic, received about 3 percent of the vote. It appeared from that vote that the majority of the people were satisfied with the commonwealth arrangement.

However, an apparently very small group continues to promote independence by terror through frequent bombings and other intimidation. The proposal by retiring President Ford in 1977 that Puerto Rico become a state as soon as possible appeared to fall flat. Apparently most of the people still like commonwealth status.

Political parties in Puerto Rico have received unusual attention. The law limits the amount of contributions individuals can make to a party in any one year. However, each recognized political party receives equal contributions from the government so that all viewpoints will have an opportunity to be heard. If a minority party gets a substantial vote but does not elect candidates to the Legislative Assembly, extra senators-at-large or representatives-at-large are allowed.

Puerto Ricans have shown an unusual interest in their government. In the election of 1964, 83.5 percent of all those eligible to vote actually voted—a far better record than on the mainland. They are serious about the responsibility they have undertaken in the words of their constitution "To enrich our democratic heritage in the individual and collective enjoyment of its rights and privileges ... for a better world based on these principles."

As former Israeli leader David Ben Gurion stated, "The commonwealth is a tribute to the political system of the United States."

THE PEOPLE

Puerto Rico is one of the world's most densely populated areas—928 persons to the square mile (358 persons per square kilometer).

Life has not been easy for the people of Puerto Rico, and yet when

Ponce de León would never recognize his "rich port"—modern San Juan.

they say to visitors *"esta es su casa"*—"this is your house"—seldom does anyone have cause to doubt that they mean just that. Family ties are strong, extending to grandparents, aunts and uncles, cousins, and even godfathers and godmothers. No matter what catastrophe happens, somewhere in this "extended family system" someone will be able to come to the rescue.

Family names are used according to the Spanish custom. The Office of the Commonwealth of Puerto Rico says, "If a man's name is Juan González Ramírez, the González stands for his father and the Ramírez for his mother. He is addressed as Mr. González. If Juan has a sister, María, she is María González Ramírez. If she marries Jorge García Velásquez, she . . . adds 'de García Velásquez.' You can address her as Mrs. García. If she has a son, José, he is José García González."

Life has improved greatly for most Puerto Ricans. In 1940 the life span was only forty-six years. In 1960, only twenty years later, it had expanded to almost seventy years. The commonwealth has the goal of a "good home for every family," and is rapidly moving forward toward realizing that goal.

The governor's palace

The number of people leaving their native island is not so large as it once was. To help those who are planning to leave or the hundreds of thousands now living in New York, Chicago, and other mainland cities, the Puerto Rican government has done what no other government ever did before. It has established a program to help Puerto Ricans and the communities in which they settle to adjust to one another, for the mutual benefit of each, as quickly as possible. This is carried out both among the people who are planning to leave and in the mainland cities where most of the others have gone.

PUERTO RICO TODAY

The ties of citizenship grew stronger during World War II when many Puerto Ricans served in the United States armed forces. Then 39,591 Puerto Rican volunteers served in the armed forces during the Korean War.

Before he left the governor's chair, Luis Muñoz Marín pointed out to the people that "Material progress is not enough." In addition to Operation Bootstrap, the government established Operation Serenidad to help the people find the "good life" in more creative ways. Work of this operation has ranged from restoration of old churches, houses, and forts to the rediscovery of folklore and old music. The Puerto Rico Symphony Orchestra, the Casals Festival, Opera and Drama Festival, and much more are all part of Operation Serenidad, which seems to be leading a "great cultural reawakening on the island."

Whatever may be the future course of Puerto Rico, it seems certain that the people will continue to operate a "showcase of democracy in action in the Caribbean."

NATURAL TREASURES

As the glowing sun sinks behind the swaying trees with their orchid-laden branches, the casual visitor to Puerto Rico is inclined to

The rare Puerto Rican Parrot is on the endangered list.

feel that here is a land of unlimited natural treasure. There is, it is true, almost unlimited natural beauty but nature has not bestowed wealth with a lavish hand in the island.

The most important Puerto Rican resource is the soil that sometimes is "spectacularly fertile." However, much of the island is too ruggedly mountainous to permit agriculture; probably less than a million acres (four hundred thousand hectares) are suitable for cultivation in all of Puerto Rico. Few mineral resources have been found; most of the gold once found there was quickly spirited away by the early Spanish. Limited supplies of manganese are found north of Juana Diaz. Limestone is plentiful for building and cement making. Gypsum, clays, and marble are in fairly good supply, and there are some supplies of granite and magnetic iron.

Magnificent forests that once blanketed most of the island now live only in the early accounts. The only virgin forest left is now preserved in the Caribbean national forest. However, the tree growth is rapid, and forests in Puerto Rico have been replaced fairly rapidly in areas not suitable for agriculture. About 88,000 acres (35,600 hectares) of forest have been established by the govern-

29

Tourists can travel from the west coast to the southeast coast over La Ruta Panorámica.

ment. A new tree of some commercial promise is the chironja. This apparently sprang from a natural cross between an orange and a grapefruit.

The slopes of El Yunque nurture a luxuriant tropical rain forest. Here grow more than two hundred species of trees. Tree ferns live up to their names by growing as high as some trees. Hardwoods, palms, and a host of flowers flourish, including many orchids. One of the island's most interesting sights is the tiny orchid with a perfect flower scarcely larger than the head of a pin.

Adding brilliant color to the deep shadows and dappled sunlight of the rain forest are the multi-hued native parrots and the dainty iridescent hummingbirds, as well as many other birds.

For those who might have some fear of the wildlife in a tropical land, there is the assurance that almost no wildlife exists on Puerto

30

Rico. The iguana and small lizards and the imported mongoose are among the few "wild" creatures found. Both the flora and the fauna of the islands seem to have come from South America, creeping up over the arc of the Lesser Antilles.

One of the most appealing little creatures anywhere is found almost throughout Puerto Rico. This is the tiny singing tree frog called *coqui*. His song, melodic as any bird's, serenades the whole island during the evening, lulling both children and adults to sleep with his pure flute-like tone. Only the males sing.

Puerto Rico's ocean waters contain a tiny and delicious variety of oyster, succulent langouste, and shrimp, and fine food fish such as snapper, kingfish, and tuna. For big game fishermen there are sailfish and giant blue marlin. Puerto Rico has held several records for blue marlin.

No one who enjoys the beauties of Puerto Rico will ever feel that the island has been shortchanged by nature. One look at such a sight as the flamboyant trees arching across the country roads in tunnels of flame is enough to convince any visitor that here is a land of wonderful charm.

THE PEOPLE USE THEIR TREASURES

"In 1940 the people of Puerto Rico resolved that poverty was intolerable." They also decided that if anything were to be done to improve their lot, they would have to do it themselves—lift themselves by their own bootstraps, and so they started "Operation Bootstrap."

To promote manufacturing, an agency called *Fomento* was established. At first Fomento built and operated factories. The factories operated at a loss, and it was feared that Puerto Rico was becoming a socialist state. However, Fomento sold its factories, which soon began to make a profit in private hands. Fomento then turned most of its attention to attracting new industries, with their new jobs, to Puerto Rico. A ten-year, tax-free period and other attractions were offered. It was pointed out that the people of Puerto Rico are quite skillful with their hands and could provide labor in many types of industries.

The result of this effort has amazed the world. In 1955 manufacturing income passed agriculture in the value of its product. In 1964 the income generated from manufacturing was eighteen times greater than in 1940.

Hundreds of new manufacturers have come to the island since the program began. Just how many new jobs have been added cannot be known exactly, but it is estimated that there have been more than two hundred fifty thousand. Some of the many well-known firms' names include American Can, Carborundum, General Electric, International Shoe, Parke-Davis, Phelps Dodge, and Union Carbide. The Commonwealth Oil Refinery Company is the largest single industrial enterprise in Puerto Rico. Today income from manufacturing is over two billion dollars.

In agriculture, the reform movement broke up the great sugar estates, permitting landless people to buy small tracts of land. For these they paid two hundred dollars per acre over a period of forty years. If there is a crop failure, the farmer can miss the payments for three years without losing his land. However, those who fail to pay because of laziness may find that the government reclaims the land promptly.

Sugar cane is still the leading single crop, with a yearly value of over fifty million dollars. The sugar-cane fields shimmer like green seas along the coastal plains. The Sugar Corporation, started in 1973, aids in the production of sugar cane. Mechanical machines are used in harvesting the sugar cane.

Livestock and animal husbandry are important in Puerto Rican agriculture. One of the most unusual Puerto Rican animals is the aristocratic *paso fino,* one of the fine-gaited horses of the world.

"Coffee of exceptional quality is grown in the cool western mountains, as steep as upside down ice cream cones. The coffee bushes rustle in the shade of fragrant orange trees." New varieties of coffee are being developed. Coffee is the second most valuable crop.

"Tobacco farmers, roped together like mountain climbers, wield their hoes on slopes of Alpine steepness" to care for the important tobacco crop. Pineapples, bananas, coconuts, melons, cucumbers, tomatoes, and a new type of sweet potato all add to the agricultural income, which now totals over 100 million dollars per year. Possibly important for the future is the acerola, the West Indian cherry, eighty times richer in vitamin C than ordinary cherries.

Commercial fishing is important, and tuna is the most valuable catch. Puerto Rico has become an important tuna canning center.

Puerto Rico is one of the great hubs of international travel. The international airport in San Juan had to undergo a seven million dollar expansion only six years after it opened in order to double the passenger capacity to keep its position as the hub of Caribbean air traffic. Ramey Air Force Base is the country's most important air defense installation in the Caribbean. Over twenty regularly scheduled airlines and many steamship companies serve Puerto Rico.

The fact that the island has good highways, covering almost every area, is a surprise to many visitors. Five daily newspapers, an excellent English language weekly and several television stations keep the people of Puerto Rico well informed.

According to the Government Development Bank for Puerto Rico, the tourist trade is the fastest growing part of the economy. "Puerto Rico has become the most popular vacation area in the Caribbean," with several million tourists spending close to a billion dollars each year, brought by airlines and a host of cruise ships to enjoy the enchantment of this land.

Visitors touring El Morro.

HUMAN TREASURES

Many authorities consider one Puerto Rican leader a leading statesman of his day. Luis Muñoz Marín has been called the "most original political thinker in the Americas." It is said that many of the people considered him in almost the same personal relationship as a father. Very probably he might have become a dictator if he had desired. Instead, after serving four terms as chief executive (1949-65), he chose not to run for governor but rather to return to the Puerto Rican Senate, where he had served before. His decision set a remarkable example of democracy in action.

Muñoz began his extraordinary career in a notable way. At the age of fourteen he entered Georgetown University in the District of Columbia. Later he became a writer and poet and published two books before entering politics.

Muñoz came from a remarkable family; his father, Luis Muñoz Rivera, was described by many as the "greatest political leader of the times." He is sometimes known as the "George Washington of Puerto Rico." Muñoz Rivera spent ten years of "dogged effort" to win from Spain in 1897 the cherished "Charter of Autonomy" that gave the island dominion status. He later became resident commissioner in Washington, and his persistence hastened reforms from the mainland.

Another political leader, Luis Ferré, has been a leading industrialist on the island. A member of a family of Ponce, a graduate of the Massachusetts Institute of Technology, Ferré became the founder of the Statehood Republican Party. He served as governor from 1968-72. In 1976, Carlos Romero Barcelo of the New Progressive Party was elected governor for a term to end in 1981.

Among the leading women of the political world must be listed the popular Doña Felisa Rincón de Gautier, who served as mayor of San Juan for twenty years.

A successful early-day leader was Marshal Alejandro O'Reilly, sent from Spain by King Carlos III. O'Reilly took the island's first census, overhauled the military establishment, traced the patterns of smuggling, and brought about several reforms.

One of the "mainlanders" most highly thought of in Puerto Rico was Rexford Tugwell. Appointed in 1941 by Franklin D. Roosevelt as governor, Tugwell was considered to have been the most helpful of the governors appointed by presidents.

The first important literary work by a native writer is thought by many to be *El Jíbaro,* by Manuel Alonso. Eugenio María de Hostos is a well-known writer and Manuel Zeno Gandía a novelist of distinction.

José Campeche is considered by many to be Puerto Rico's finest artist. Francisco Oller, another island artist, is distinguished by the hanging of his *L'Etudiant* in the Louvre in Paris. Only one mainland United States artist has had this recognition. Julio Rosado is another fine painter and Lindsey Daen a sculptor of note.

In music, the *Danzas* of Juan Morell Campos are still enjoyed around the world. However, Puerto Rico is probably most proud of her adopted son, the famed cellist, composer, conductor Pablo Casals. The maestro's mother was born in Puerto Rico, and he returned there when he could no longer tolerate conditions in his native Spain. "When I came here," Casals recalled, "I told Governor Muñoz Marín that I could not become just an old man who is retiring. I told him, 'Here or anywhere, I need music.'" So at the age of eighty he founded the international Casals Festival and helped Puerto Rico music in an infinite number of ways until his death in San Juan in 1973.

TEACHING AND LEARNING

One of the outstanding recent accomplishments of the people of Puerto Rico has been in education. In less than fifteen years most of the people became literate where before the large majority were not. By plowing 25 to 30 percent of the commonwealth's budget into education, Puerto Rico was able by 1957 to provide a basic elementary education for all children of elementary age. Enrollment in public and private schools in 1940 was 286,113—now it is about eight hundred thousand.

Spanish is the mother tongue, but English is spoken quite generally, and the aim of the schools is to teach English to all students, in addition to Spanish.

There are seven institutions of higher education in Puerto Rico. The vast University of Puerto Rico with an enrollment of thirty-five thousand must be considered one of the great universities of the hemisphere. It was founded in 1903 and has sprawling campuses in Rio Piedras, a suburb of San Juan, at Mayagüez and Cayey. One of the notable parts of the university is its new Institute for Caribbean Studies. It supports a School of Tropical Medicine, a School for Cooperatives, and an Institute of Labor Relations. The Center for Nuclear Studies on the Mayagüez campus serves all Latin America.

The Inter American University of Puerto Rico is also at San Juan. The Catholic University at Ponce was established in 1948. Other institutions of higher learning are the College of the Sacred Heart, San Juan; Ana G. Méndez Educational Foundation, Turabo University College, Caguas; and Bayamón Central University, Bayamón. University enrollment has jumped from thirteen thousand in 1950 to over sixty thousand in the '70s.

The Metropolitan Vocational School of San Juan, with over three thousand students, is one of the largest and most outstanding of its type anywhere. The Free Schools of Music at San Juan, Ponce, and Mayagüez, and the High School for Music are outstanding. In 1960 a new Conservatory of Music opened, with Pablo Casals as director and famed concert artist Jesús María Sanroma on the piano faculty.

In a sense, all of Puerto Rico might be considered a "school." More than twenty-three thousand observers and investigators have come to the island from one hundred twenty-six counties, especially the underdeveloped countries, to study methods used by the islanders to shake off their historic poverty—technicians to learn how Puerto Ricans are taught to be skilled industrial workers, teachers to see how adults learn to read and write, economists eager to understand how the economy of Puerto Rico was transformed, among others. Puerto Ricans sometimes complain that their accomplishments are much better known throughout the world than they are on the mainland of the United States.

36

The elegant administration building of the University of Puerto Rico.

ENCHANTMENT OF PUERTO RICO

"Land of glistening palm fringed beaches, vivid green mountains, sun and trade winds, of ancient grey Spanish fortresses contrasting with concrete and glass hotels, of churches and modern factories" — that is the land of Puerto Rico being discovered by a constantly growing throng of tourists.

Here is a striking mingling of Spanish and United States customs. For example, baseball is the number one sport, and many Big League baseball players have come from Puerto Rico, among them Orlando Cepeda, 1958 Rookie of the Year and 1959 Sophomore of the Year, and Roberto Clemente, one of the greatest baseball players, who died in a plane crash off the coast of Puerto Rico when flying to the aid of earthquake victims in Nicaragua.

On the other hand, fiestas are still popular. The Spanish customs

37

of the Christmas season are lengthy and popular. The season extends from early December to January 8. Much of the old world atmosphere is still found in the smaller towns such as Hormigueros, Cabo Rojo, and Barranquitas. Here there is almost a detachment from the twentieth century.

Every town was built around a plaza, generally picturesque. Every town has its patron saint, such as the town of Loiza Aldea, which chose St. Patrick, who supposedly drove the snakes out of Ireland. St. Patrick is said to have done a similar favor for Loiza Aldea by driving out the ants when the town was stricken with a plague of them.

In Puerto Rico mainlanders find many activities not permitted in most other parts of the country. Cockfights are legal and very popular. Fortunately, the "pampered creatures with their iridescent feathers" are seldom killed in their fierce battles, and they sometimes sell for hundreds of dollars. Puerto Rico also has legal lotteries.

Wonderful climate, fishing, swimming, sightseeing, and the many cultural events often combine to make people who come to the island seek to buy a permanent home before their vacation is over.

OLDEST CITY: SAN JUAN

In San Juan Bautista de Puerto Rico, visitors have the privilege of seeing the oldest permanently inhabited European settlement under the United States flag. Some of the original foundations still stand, including those believed to have supported the house of Juan Ponce de León, first governor.

Casa Blanca (White House), in San Juan, is the oldest continuously inhabited European home in the Western Hemisphere. It survived five major wartime sieges, as well as earthquakes and hurricanes. About 230 acres (93 hectares) of old San Juan, which occupied about four blocks of an island, are being restored by the Puerto Rican Institute of Culture in much the same careful and impressive manner as colonial Williamsburg, Virginia.

Casa Blanca

One of the most impressively beautiful structures in the Western Hemisphere is the gleaming white bulk of La Fortaleza. Constructed in 1533 as a governor's palace, it is the oldest executive mansion still used for its original purpose in the hemisphere. As other governors have for over four hundred years, today's governor still lives in the graceful building, which has been completely restored at a cost of five hundred thousand dollars.

Glowering over the harbor, still giving the impression of great dignity and force, towers the mass of El Morro, the mighty Spanish fortress. Its even mightier partner, San Cristobal, was considered the most powerfully fortified base in the hemisphere.

San Juan Cathedral is said to be "one of the finest examples of Spanish colonial architecture in the New World."

The imposing capitol building of Puerto Rico at San Juan is built along the clean-cut lines of the Italian renaissance. The building was dedicated July 17, 1925. It is decorated with fine mosaics and art work of such artists as Rafael Rios Rey, José R. Oliver, and Jorge Rechani y Rafael Tufiño.

The capitol in San Juan.

The contrast in San Juan between the very old and the very new is great. The supreme court building is a striking, modern structure. Modern San Juan has almost exploded outward until it covers 30 square miles (78 square kilometers) and overflows into surrounding areas such as Santurce. The tourist pier of San Juan has been completely reconditioned. The striking resort structures of the Gold Coast remind tourists of Miami Beach. And yet tourists can also stay in some of the very old buildings, such as the ancient convent restored and converted by R.F. Woolworth to make a hotel now known as El Convento.

In spring and early summer one of the most renowned events of the musical world is the Casals Festival, attracting thousands of music-loving visitors. From March to May, Broadway hits visit the Tapia Theater. In fall concerts of the Puerto Rico Symphony are performed, and the city has thriving ballet and theater groups.

OTHER ISLAND ATTRACTIONS

Those who never get beyond San Juan in their exploration of the

40

island are missing much of the charm and real life of Puerto Rico and a great deal that is most typical of the island and island life.

Ponce is the third city of Puerto Rico. Someone has said that "Ponce is to San Juan what Boston is to New York." Perched on the blue-green Caribbean, Ponce too has its ultra modern El Ponce Intercontinental Hotel, a striking white and blue structure overlooking the sea. One of the finer art museums anywhere is the Ponce Museum of Art, founded by industrialist Luis U. Ferré.

Mayagüez is a sunny, booming port on the west coast. San Germán is the second oldest settlement on the island. Ancient Porta Coeli Church built by missionaries in 1606 sits on a knoll overlooking the plaza in San Germán. It now serves as a museum. Facing it across the plaza is the "new church"—only two hundred years old.

Parguera Bay near the southwest corner of the island is world renowned for its phosphoresence. Small organisms make the waters appear to glow with fire with every movement or ripple. Fish gliding through the luminous sea glow like tracer bullets.

Arecibo is renowned for the world's largest radar telescope ionospheric observatory. The Dorado Beach Hotel, built by Laurance S. Rockefeller, has been called "the most luxurious place on the island."

Almost anywhere the visitor turns, in following the roads of the island, is something interesting or beautiful.

Mile upon mile of shoreline is edged by gleaming beaches—one of these, Luquillo, is backed by a veritable rampart of waving palm trees. Completely contrasting are the mountain areas. The most spectacular of these is the glistening tropical rain forest manteling the mountain El Yunque. Here about sixteen hundred rain showers fall every year, totalling 180 inches (4.5 meters). Blossoms of red and other brilliant colors, squawking parrots, multitudes of orchids, fern fronds towering as tall as 30 feet (9 meters), all help to transport the visitor to this paradise into another world.

In fact, many visitors feel that Puerto Ricans enjoy the best of two worlds—the old and the new. Here, as one visitor comments, is "one of the most exciting places to live and visit that can be found anywhere on earth."

A queen angelfish swims amid coral in Buck Island Reef National Monument near St. Croix.

Virgin Islands of the United States

LAY OF THE LAND

Depending on how you count, there are about one hundred islands and islets in the Virgin Islands. Of these, sixty-five are in the American group, but only three are of major importance—St. Croix, St. Thomas, and St. John. These three total 128 square miles (332 kilometers) in area, with St. Croix about two thirds of the total size.

St. Croix is about 40 miles (64 kilometers) south of St. Thomas. The Virgin Islands are the westernmost islands of the Lesser Antilles, and they are the northeast "outpost" of the Caribbean. The eastern tip of St. Croix forms the most easterly part of the United States. St. Croix is 1,434 miles (2,308 kilometers) from New York and 991 miles (1,595 kilometers) from Miami. Puerto Rico is the nearest neighbor, and some geographers call the Virgin Islands "satellites" of Puerto Rico.

The islands are the tops of extinct volcanic mountain peaks, based on submarine plateaus. St. Thomas and St. John are on the same plateau; between those two and St. Croix the bottom of the sea plummets to the incredible depth of 15,000 feet (4,572 meters). The magnificent harbor of St. Thomas is one of the few good harbors in the Caribbean.

It is said the "climate of the islands is as nearly perfect as climate can be," with the balmy trade winds supplying the "air conditioning." In fact, the weather is "guaranteed." Hotels and guest houses take out insurance policies and give guests their rooms free on any day the mean temperature drops below 70 degrees Fahrenheit (21.1 degrees Celsius), which hasn't happened in twenty-five years. The average rainfall is 46.3 inches (118 centimeters), but evaporation is high.

YESTERDAY AND TODAY

The first known inhabitants of the Virgin Islands were the Siboney

Indians, who apparently moved there from Florida. They were driven out by the Arawak, a peace-loving group who arrived from South America by way of the chain of the Lesser Antilles. These people knew how to make ceramic pieces, clubs, and bows and arrows. They appear to have invented the hammock. Columbus first tried these swinging beds in his ships, and sailors, as well as landlubbers, have been delighting in them ever since.

Columbus gave the islands their names in honor of the eleven thousand virgins of St. Ursula, who left Britain for a fifth-century crusade to the Holy Land. When Columbus discovered the Virgin Islands on his second voyage (1493), he found the fierce Carib tribesmen living there. It is thought they had come only about one hundred years before that time and had driven out most of the Arawak.

The Carib attacked Columbus with poisoned arrows, and killed one of his men. They delighted in eating human flesh, and Columbus called them *Caníbales,* from which the word cannibal comes. The Carib people showed little fear of the Europeans, and it is thought they may only have considered them as a change of diet.

The Carib lived in palm-thatched huts, ate wood rats, among other things, and when food was scarce they ate their dogs, which were of an interesting, voiceless breed. They made beer from sweet potatoes or corn and inhaled tobacco smoke until they collapsed.

By 1596 the islands were almost completely uninhabited. No one knows what happened to the Carib, but it is thought the islands were depopulated by slave hunts.

In 1642 the Dutch planted Nieuw Zeeland, the first colony on the islands. The Spanish used the islands as assembly points for their treasure ships, which often played a grim kind of hide and seek with pirates who thrived on the islands. Captain Kidd and the swashbuckling Henry Morgan found shelter there, and the notorious Bluebeard built his legendary tower there, where he is said to have kept and murdered his many wives.

The flags of Spain, Holland, France, England, Denmark, and the United States have flown over the Virgin Islands. In 1651 St. Croix was bought by the French Chevalier du Bois for the Knights of Malta organization. Du Bois built a great palace with formal gardens on St. Croix, but the organization's efforts failed after he died.

By 1733 when Denmark purchased St. Croix from the French, Denmark was in control of all the Virgin Islands. The Danish people created a great and flourishing civilization on the islands, using hordes of slaves to cultivate the sugar cane. The islands became the "sugar bowl of Europe." Great plantation houses with every luxury were built, surrounded by splendid gardens. Good roads led to all parts of the main islands.

In 1840 the city of St. Thomas (now Charlotte Amalie) was the third largest in the Danish empire. Then the slaves were freed; the market for sugar dropped and the islands began a rapid decline.

The United States first tried to buy the islands just after the Civil War. But the commission's ship was hurled on the shore of St. Croix by a tidal wave, and the deal fell through. At last in 1917 the Danish government sold the Virgin Islands to the United States for twenty-five million dollars. It was feared that if the United States did not buy them Germany would do so and acquire a base in the Western Hemisphere during World War I.

The people of the islands were made United States citizens in 1927. A form of limited self-government was set up in 1936 and expanded in 1954. The islands are classified as "organized unincorporated territory" of the United States.

More than 80 percent of the people of the islands are wholly or partly descendants of the slaves who worked the Danish plantations. People of French origin have lived in the islands for many generations. Persons of Scottish, Spanish, and Portuguese descent are also found. Then there is an increasing group from the United States mainland and nearby Puerto Rico who have found the islands to be the paradise they are seeking.

NATURAL TREASURES

The contrast between the leeward and the windward sides of the islands is striking. On St. Croix the visitor can progress from a region of cactus and iguanas to lush tropical woodland in the short 24 mile (38.6 kilometer) extent of the island.

One of the world's rarest birds, the bare-legged owl, is a ghostly inhabitant of the islands. This species has been spotted only twice in the last 50 years. Although among the world's tiniest birds, the Antillean crested hummingbird will fiercely attack the largest hawk and often put him to rout. The largest island bird is the mammoth frigate bird, king of the air. The great blue heron, pelicans, and the dainty honey creeper are other birds.

The only native mammals are bats, including the strange fishing bats. Virginia or white-tailed deer were imported to the islands for hunting, and the pesky mongoose is another imported creature.

Coconut and royal palms abound, and the undeveloped shores are lined with mangrove, mahoe, and sea grape trees. Exotic fruit trees include the mango, lime, avocado, papaya, soursop, guava, sugar apple, genep, and mammee. The kapok tree grows with huge gnarled and twisted roots above the ground, and furnishes fluffy stuffing for pillows.

The game fish of Virgin Island waters are remarkable. An officially recorded blue marlin was captured in 1977—1,282 pounds (582 kilograms). Tuna, wahoo, tarpon, kingfish, and bonefish are taken year round. In the crystal-clear waters, beautiful coral fish dart and glide, including such fluorescent wonders as the marine jewel. Among others are French angelfish, queen angel, rock beauty, and yellowtail. The islands are a shell hunter's paradise with six hundred fifty different species. A hundred of these are rare to very rare.

Local building materials come from the stone, sand, and gravel of the islands, but there are no minerals in commercial quantities.

The greatest resource problem of the islands is fresh water. There are no lakes or rivers and almost no sources of fresh underground water for wells. Runoff water from rains supplies most of the water, and every house is required to have a cistern. Concrete catch basins are seen everywhere. A desalting plant for seawater completed on St. Thomas in 1962 helps by providing a supply of 275,000 gallons (1,041,000 liters) of fresh water daily, but water shortages will continue to be a problem.

Snorkeling in clear, clean water near St. John.

THE PEOPLE USE THEIR TREASURES

Much progress has been made in the Virgin Islands since Herbert Hoover was forced to call them "an effective poorhouse." Agriculture is still the second most important source of income, but this is limited to a few small valleys. At one time 259 sugar mills were converting the cane crop, and the old stone mill towers used for grinding the cane dot the island, even now. Of course, cane is still an important crop. Much of this is now converted into rum, the principal present-day industry of the islands.

Bay rum is made from the bay leaf, and the fine quality of the islands' bay oil makes it important to perfume and cosmetic manufacturers. Another tree, the divi-divi, is also useful; it provides an excellent source of tannin for leathers. Handbags and straw hats are woven by the French hat makers from the strands of the bull tyre palms.

The Virgin Islands Corporation is a government company designed to develop the economy of the islands.

Since 1964 the most important source of income of the Virgin Islands has been the tourist trade. The annual income from tourists is more than four times as much as the total paid by the United States for the islands.

Instead of being among the lowest in income of the area, the people of the United States Virgin Islands now have achieved the highest per capita income in the Caribbean.

TEACHING AND LEARNING

The literacy rate of the Virgin Islands is about comparable to that of the mainland. Public education covers kindergarten through high school, and St. Thomas has a vocational secondary school.

In 1964 a long column of people in academic robes walked across a St. Thomas golf course. This was a procession honoring the inauguration of the first president of the College of the Virgin Islands and was the first academic procession ever to take place there. The college was founded in 1963, with campuses on St. Thomas and St. Croix.

ENCHANTMENT OF THE VIRGIN ISLANDS

There is a kind of "storybook picturesqueness" about the Virgin Islands. The old-world background is more apparent here than in any other part of the United States. Here also is some of the world's prime scenery, such as Trunk Bay on St. John, one of the ten most beautiful beaches in the Western Hemisphere.

The water around the islands is indescribably clear, and magnificent underwater formations may be seen in such places as Buck Island Reef National Monument, an unusual underwater trail.

Festivals on the island are particularly interesting with their wild costumes, the famous drum bands, and the impossible twists and angles of the limbs. Christmas festival on St. Croix and the April-Ending Carnival of St. Croix are among the most impressive. Transfer Day on March 31 celebrates the transfer of the islands to the United States.

The beauty of the harbor of Charlotte Amalie, named for a Danish queen, has been said to "beggar description." It is one of the world's ranking ports of call for cruise ships. The town's quaint streets bear such romantic names as Jasmine Lane, Orchid Row, and Hibiscus Alley. Skyline Drive gives a magnificent view of the city and of the islet-dotted harbor below. One vantage point on the drive rises to 1,200 feet (366 meters).

One of the most interesting sections of Charlotte Amalie is the district where the sturdy old warehouses have been converted into a most unusual shopping center. Here fine merchandise from all over the world attracts buyers. Shops of the islands rank among the most famous in the world. Flags of the United States and the Virgin Islands fly over the candy-pink administration building with its delicate white wrought-iron balconies. During Danish times it was a stately colonial mansion.

All Saints Episcopal Church was built by parishioners who used

Three Kings Day Celebration on St. Croix

molasses to mix the mortar because of a shortage of water. Frederick Evangelical Lutheran Church is the second oldest Lutheran Church in the Western Hemisphere, and the St. Thomas Synagog may be the oldest Jewish congregation under the United States flag.

Fort Christian, now a national historic site, is the oldest building still in use in the islands. Bluebeard's Castle, the Crystal Palace, and many other historic old buildings may be seen on St. Thomas.

St. Croix is the home of two colorful towns, Christiansted and Frederiksted. The wharf area of Christiansted has been designated a national historic site. The old Steeple Building has been restored by the National Park Service and is now a fine museum which houses Carib and Arawak relics among other treasures. Visitors strolling down the arcaded sidewalks may still trade at the hardware store where Alexander Hamilton clerked as a very young man.

Picturesque ruins of the old plantations are reminders of the almost incredible culture and civilization achieved by Denmark in this remote spot. Some of them have been restored.

One of the principal attractions of St. John is the Virgin Islands National Park, dedicated there in 1956 as the nation's twenty-ninth national park.

Wherever the visitor goes in the Virgin Islands, he is reminded of the truth of the name that the islands' own people use for their homeland—"Islands of Contentment."

Panama Canal

LAY OF THE LAND

Between the years 1903 and 1979, an area of land on either side of the canal was governed by the United States. The strip of land, extending about 5 miles (8 kilometers) from both sides of the canal for its entire length, was called the Panama Canal Zone. For years, U.S. management of the Zone angered the people of Panama and some other Latin American countries. In 1979, President Carter's lengthy battle to return control of the old zone to the Panamanians finally concluded.

The biggest surprise about the Panama Canal is that it does not "run" east and west. Because of the way the Isthmus curves, the length of the canal stretches from northwest on the Caribbean side to southeast on the Pacific side, at the Bay of Panama.

In past times the Isthmus of Panama was cut by a strait, a gash of water separating the two continents. Movements of the earth's crust raised the sea bottom, joining the continents and separating the oceans. The geology of the area gives evidence of volcanic action.

The land is ruggedly mountainous, including the Continental Divide. The mountains are covered with tropical vegetation, encouraged by annual rainfall from 70 to 140 inches (178 to 356 centimeters). The temperature rarely rises above 90 degrees Fahrenheit (32.2 degrees Celsius), but it seldom falls below 70 degrees Fahrenheit (21.1 degrees Celsius). Part of the time refreshing trade winds blow, but often the region suffers in the doldrums. The chief obstacle to any major effort in the region is the enervating climate.

YESTERDAY AND TODAY

The Isthmus of Panama was one of the first parts of the American mainland discovered. Rodrigo de Bastidas discovered the coast in 1501. Columbus landed in 1502. In 1510 Vasco Nuñez de Balboa arrived in the region, known as Darien, to take control. He made friends with the Indians. In 1513 he persuaded them to embark with him on the long and dangerous expedition to explore the interior.

Finally in one of the historic moments of all time, Balboa stood on his "Peak in Darien" and became the first European to discover the Pacific Ocean. He claimed it and all the shores washed by it in the name of the King of Spain. From that time on it was clear that only about 40 miles (64 kilometers) of mountainous terrain separated the two oceans.

For more than three hundred years the isthmus was crossed by pack trains on a rocky trail. The gold and silver and other wealth of the Spanish possessions in South America were carried along this trail. Freebooters such as Sir Francis Drake attacked the wealth-laden caravans and often made off with fabulous booty.

After gold was discovered in California, thousands of gold seekers sailed to Panama, made their way across the isthmus and took another boat to California. A fortune in California gold was also brought back across the Isthmus. By 1855 the tremendous feat of building a railroad, the first one to cross the continent, was accomplished by a group of New York financiers. The route between the oceans was made much more reliable by the Panama Railroad Company.

Ever since Charles V of Spain first thought about the idea in 1523 and Alvaro de Saavedra drew the first plans, men had dreamed of a canal across the isthmus. Quantities of freight could be carried by boat with tremendous savings over going around the tip of South America or transporting it across the land of the isthmus. ·

The first to dare the monumental task was Ferdinand de Lesseps. He felt that his experience in building the Suez Canal would make the task in Panama relatively easy. However, even the opening ceremony failed to go right. After twenty years of almost incredible hardships, the French Compagnie Universelle du Canal Interoceanique was defeated by deadly disease and financial woes.

The United States, under Theodore Roosevelt, took an interest in the canal. Panama at this time was part of Colombia, even though Panamanians had proclaimed their independence in 1830, 1831, and 1840. When Colombia refused to ratify a treaty for the United States to construct the canal, the people of Panama again revolted and on

November 3, 1903, set up a separate country. Many of the countries of Latin America still feel that the United States was responsible for the revolt in Panama. The French company encouraged leading Panama families to separate the country from Colombia, because the French were to receive forty million dollars for their part of the canal work, although this was less than a sixth of their loss.

The new Republic of Panama granted to the United States all rights and power within a new Panama Canal Zone, and the United States began to build. On October 10, 1913, President Woodrow Wilson pressed a button, and the waters of the two oceans flooded together. On August 15, 1914, the first ship, the SS *Ancon*, passed from ocean to ocean through the new Panama Canal.

The military importance of the canal was illustrated during World War II when 5,300 combat vessels and 8,500 other craft serving military needs were locked through.

On January 9 and 10, 1964, in what began as a clash of high school students, mobs of Panamanians clashed with United States troops. Twenty-five were killed and three hundred fifty injured. Panama demanded that the treaty with the United States be revised with more favorable terms for Panama.

In April, 1978, after much debate and urging from President Jimmy Carter, the United States Senate approved two Panama Canal treaties. One turns complete control of the canal over to Panama in stages until 2000. The other gives both Panama and the United States the right to defend the waterway after December 31, 1999.

In a *Time* magazine article written in 1982, former President Jimmy Carter explained why he fought to ratify the treaties returning control of the canal and the Canal Zone to the Panamanians.

The treaty that established the Canal Zone and gave the United States the right to complete the canal that the French had begun was signed on November 18, 1903, little more than two weeks after the Panamanian revolt. According to President Carter, no Panamanian ever saw a copy of the treaty until after it was signed. Acting on behalf of Panama was a French businessman. The Frenchman demanded that the Panamanian government comply with the new agreement or face extinction.

When President Carter took office in 1976, he made it one of his primary duties to right what he considered to be a political wrong. In October of 1979, American flags throughout the Canal Zone were lowered as Panamanian flags were raised. The Canal Zone was no longer. Many Americans who had lived and worked in the zone remarked bitterly that President Carter had "given away" the canal. Ronald Reagan, who would defeat Jimmy Carter in the 1980 election, heartily agreed with them.

BUILDING THE CANAL

Building the Panama Canal has been called "one of the richest sagas of United States history." The French had spent $260,000,000 and untold lives, and much of this work was useful to the United States. However, the French had planned a sea level canal, and the United States decided that locks, to raise ships a part of the way, would save a tremendous amount of earth moving.

Even then the total excavation exceeded 200,000,000 cubic yards (152,911,000 cubic meters), enough to make 100 pyramids the size of the great Pyramid of Cheops. However, before this could be done the unhealthy conditions of the area had to be improved.

When the Americans came in, deaths from yellow fever soared. By spring of 1905 more than 90 percent of the American force had fled. Then Colonel William C. Gorgas arrived. Few people believed him when he said that mosquitoes caused yellow fever, but he persisted. For a time more of the digging force was working to eliminate the mosquitoes than on the canal. Concrete culverts were cast and swamps were drained; oil was burned in ditches; marshes were saturated with oil to smother them in their breeding places; potent mosquito killers were mixed and sprayed everywhere.

The results were almost unbelievable. By September, 1905, Gorgas defeated the dread yellowjack. In that month, Dr. Gorgas entered a room in Ancon Hospital where a man had just died of yellow fever. "Take a good look at this man," he told the doctors, "For that is the last case of yellow fever. . . There will never be any more death from this cause in Panama." The prophecy has stood.

Work went on; the Continental Divide was sliced asunder. The great locks, 1,000 feet (305 meters) long and 110 feet (34 meters) wide, were constructed. Each leaf (door) of the two at each end of a lock is 7 feet (2 meters) thick, 65 feet (20 meters) wide and up to 82 feet (25 meters) tall. These mighty doors move with the precision of a fine watch. Construction work was done so well that many of the original parts of the canal mechanisms are still in perfect condition. Rivers were dammed and artificial lakes built to provide the enormous amount of water required to operate the locks. Fifty-two million gallons (196,841,000 liters) of water are needed for each ship. This is all fed in by gravity; there are no pumps.

The initial cost of the canal was $362,000,000. Since it was opened, there have been many additions, enlargements and improvements. Gross investment in the canal has been $1,600,000,000—all without a whisper of graft or corruption. Of this, $1,100,000,000 has already been recovered through the operation of the canal. All phases of that operation require a staff of 15,000 people.

In 1979, as required by the new treaties, the government of Panama took control over the majority of land around the canal. Over the next two and a half years, Panama would gradually begin controlling the courts and the police.

The new treaties also specified that the U.S. would retain control over a portion of the old zone (about 40 percent of the total area) in order to maintain military bases to secure the vital waterway linking the Atlantic and Pacific oceans.

Although some American politicians predicted chaos on the canal as Panama gradually assumed its management, the dire predictions have so far been unfulfilled. In fact, by 1983 the canal was earning more money than ever and the number of ships passing through it had increased from an average of 38 to 42 daily.

Nevertheless, some people worry that the Panamanian government is unstable and may yet cause catastrophic disruptions in canal operations. Should the country of Panama ever turn hostile toward the United States, the U.S. government estimates that it would take 100,000 armed soldiers to keep the canal open for ships from the United States and other friendly nations.

HUMAN TREASURES

Three men have been particularly noteworthy in the building of the canal: John F. Stevens, chief engineer; Colonel George W. Goethals, in charge after the army took over, and Dr. William Crawford Gorgas.

Stevens took charge during the early part of the effort; he restored the Isthmus railroad which was essential to the building, and he built up the organization necessary to complete the work. It is said that he was "beloved of his men."

When Stevens left the work, the Army Corps of Engineers under Colonel Goethals was placed in charge. No detail escaped his attention; he was a dominant figure. He sometimes was ruthless, but always fair. He was never too busy to listen to the complaint of an employee. On Sunday mornings in a suite of the Tivoli Hotel he heard anyone who had a grievance or a problem. Construction moved at a rapid pace.

This would not have been possible, however, without the vision of Dr. Gorgas. With little official cooperation, he buried Panama's reputation as the grave of the white man. "He had made the land sweet, and countless people owed their lives to him." He played a key role in the canal; "he was a soldier, a doctor, a humanitarian. The good he did will live to bless the peoples of the world in generations unborn." When Dr. Gorgas died in 1920, he was a world hero.

No listing of key figures in the building of the canal can be made without mention of the president of the United States who fought at home and abroad to get it started and was responsible for encouraging the swift completion of the work—Theodore Roosevelt.

ENCHANTMENT OF THE PANAMA CANAL

One of the great thrills of a trip through the canal is the lifting of the ship 85 feet (26 meters) with no noticeable motion or disturbance in the giant water stairways of the locks. When the boat enters Miraflores Locks, linemen in rowboats come up to attach tow lines

from the ship to the electric mules (locomotives). After the ship is safely in the lock, the 700-ton (635-metric ton) gates, 82 (25 meters) feet tall, slowly begin to close, leaving the ship in the depths of an enormous, open cavern. Then the water floods in, and the ship slowly rises to the next level.

Probably the most monumental part of the canal construction was the "Big Ditch" where the Continental Divide had to be cut. This used to be known as Culebra Cut. Later the name was changed to honor Colonel D. Gaillard, engineer in charge of the work.

Soon the ship comes to Gatun Lake. The Chagres River was dammed to make the lake which at that time was the largest artificial body of water in the world. When the water of the lake rose, Barro

Colorado Island was formed. Wildlife fled to this high ground, and the area became a natural wild life preserve.

The section of the canal passing through Gatun Lake is 23 miles (37 kilometers) long. The town that is passed is Gatun. As one enters Gatun Locks, the Gatun Dam may be seen. When built, it was the largest earth-dam ever made, and many engineers felt it would never be stable. It is a mile and a half (2.4 kilometers) long and almost a half-mile (.8 kilometer) wide at the base. The trip from Gatun Locks to Cristobal Harbor, a distance of seven miles (11 kilometers), is made at sea level through a flat swampy area.

A trip through the canal is a fascinating one, but even those who pass through the canal will never be able to appreciate all the wonders that were accomplished in creating what is one of the most important traffic arteries of the world.

Navassa Island

Columbus discovered Navassa, and lost some of his party there. Americans rediscovered Navassa shortly before the Civil War. It was bonded as a guano island in 1860. The basis of the U.S. claim is the Guano Act of 1856, which said that any uninhabited island bearing the bird deposits, called guano, might be claimed peaceably for the United States by American citizens who discovered it.

The Corn Islands, Roncador Cay, Serrana Bank, Quita Suena Bank, Serranilla Bank, and the Swan Islands were formerly claimed or administered by the United States. However, the United States recently surrendered its claim to them.

The island is 30 miles (48 kilometers) west of Haiti and 75 miles (121 kilometers) northeast of Jamaica. It is about 2 miles (3 kilometers) long and 1 mile (1.6 kilometers) wide. Covered with pitfalls and thick brush, Navassa rises to a height of 250 feet (76 meters). A few poorly fed wild goats exist there.

In 1916 a presidential proclamation declared it to be under the sole jurisdiction of the United States and reserved for a lighthouse. It was put under the control of the Coast Guard, the only territory administed by that branch of service. The lonely post was a difficult spot for lighthouse keepers. One died and one went insane; finally the light was made automatic. It is serviced by Coast Guard ships at regular intervals. In 1948 vandals stripped the lighthouse.

Photo on following two pages: Runways on Sand Island, Midway Island.

AMERICA
IN THE
PACIFIC

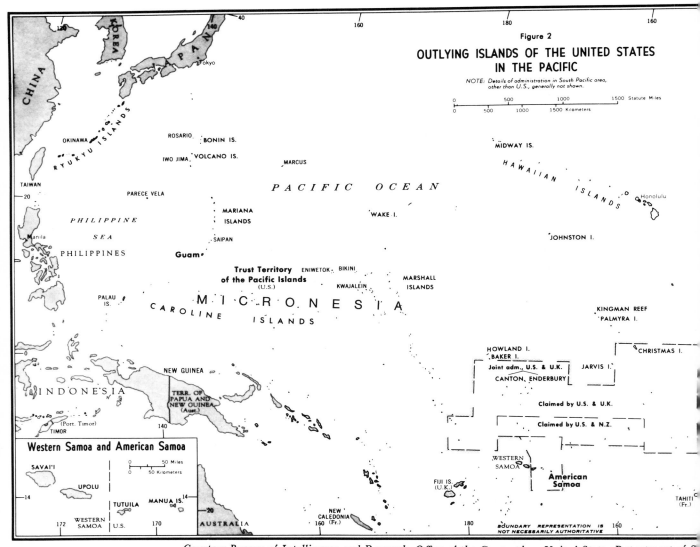

Figure 2

OUTLYING ISLANDS OF THE UNITED STATES
IN THE PACIFIC

NOTE: *Details of administration in South Pacific area,*
other than U.S., generally not shown.

CHINA
KOREA
JAPAN
Tokyo
OKINAWA
RYUKYU ISLANDS
ROSARIO
BONIN IS.
IWO JIMA
VOLCANO IS.
MARCUS
TAIWAN
PARECE VELA
PACIFIC OCEAN
MARIANA ISLANDS
WAKE I.
PHILIPPINE SEA
SAIPAN
Manila
PHILIPPINES
Guam
MIDWAY IS.
HAWAIIAN ISLANDS
Honolulu
JOHNSTON I.

Trust Territory of the Pacific Islands (U.S.)
ENIWETOK
BIKINI
KWAJALEIN
MARSHALL ISLANDS
PALAU IS.
MICRONESIA
CAROLINE ISLANDS
KINGMAN REEF
PALMYRA I.

NEW GUINEA
INDONESIA
TERR. OF PAPUA AND NEW GUINEA (Aust.)
(Port. Timor)
TIMOR

HOWLAND I.
BAKER I.
Joint adm., U.S. & U.K.
CANTON, ENDERBURY
JARVIS I.
CHRISTMAS I.

Claimed by U.S. & U.K.
Claimed by U.S. & N.Z.

WESTERN SAMOA
American Samoa
FIJI IS. (U.K.)
NEW CALEDONIA (Fr.)
AUSTRALIA
TAHITI (Fr.)

BOUNDARY REPRESENTATION IS NOT NECESSARILY AUTHORITATIVE

Western Samoa and American Samoa

SAVAI'I
UPOLU
TUTUILA
MANUA IS.
WESTERN SAMOA
U.S.

Courtesy Bureau of Intelligence and Research, Office of the Geographer, United States Department of S

Guam—Gateway to the Orient

LAY OF THE LAND

Visitors to Guam can easily climb the highest mountain in the world—37,800 feet (11,521 meters). Mount Lamlam rises only 1,334 feet (407 meters) above the sea, but it is the visible top of a volcano that extends to the awesome depth of 36,466 feet (11,115 meters) to the ocean floor. Guam is near two of the greatest depths in all the oceans.

Guam is the westernmost territory administered by the United States. Because it is west of the International Date line, it is known as the land "where America's day begins." The island lies 3,300 miles (5,311 kilometers) west of Honolulu, 1,600 miles (2,575 kilometers) east of Manila, and 1,475 miles (2,374 kilometers) south of Japan. It is the largest and most southerly of the Mariana Islands and the only one of the Marianas that is officially a territory of the United States. Guam is 30 miles (48 kilometers) long and 4 to 8.5 miles (6.4 to 13.7 kilometers) wide—the largest island between Hawaii and the Philippines. Someone has said it is shaped like a kidney bean.

It is a land of rocky headlands and golden beaches, partially enclosed by a coral reef. Within the protection of the reef the sea is jade colored; beyond, in the middle depth, a dramatic blue, blending into the deep purples of the ocean.

Forty small streams cascade down its steep slopes from the mountains. The climate is almost perfect from December through March and that of a typical tropical summer from then on.

This "gateway to the Orient" is supposed by geologists to be about twenty-five million years old.

YESTERDAY AND TODAY

Was there once in the Pacific a great continent with a wonderful and flourishing culture supporting millions of people, who became a drowned civilization when the lands sank below the sea? No one knows, but many of the ancient objects found on Guam seem to tie in with different objects found on other islands thousands of miles away, and some authorities hold to the great, lost continent theory.

Among unusual prehistoric items found on Guam are the "Latte" stones—huge carved columns, some larger than the stones of the pyramids of Egypt. These are topped with large carved mushroom-shaped stones. Their double rows are always placed parallel to a running stream or the ocean shore. Skeletons of giant-size people, rock carvings, and ancient artifacts have been found near the Lattes. More than two hundred of these sites have been found on Guam. The natives of the olden times knew nothing about where these Lattes came from, but held them in great fear and awe. Legends of the island tell of giant ancestors who may have built them.

No one has any exact information about these stone-age Latte people. It is thought that Guam was more recently occupied, since about 1500 B.C., by people who migrated from southern Asia.

When Europeans first arrived, they found the island occupied by natives calling themselves Chamorro. They lived a free and easy life with few hardships. Property was passed on through the mothers in a matriarchal system. They practiced monogamy, and there was a strict caste system. They were particularly known for their strong sense of honesty. They made and used stone mortars and pestles, adzes, chisels, pottery, bone awls, and spearheads. The men wore breech cloths and the women, grass skirts. They made sleek outrigger canoes, and their skill in navigating these was a wonder to behold.

Into this island paradise on March 6, 1521, came huge "canoes" borne along by white clouds. Ferdinand Magellan and his men had been at sea for ninety-eight days from the coast of South America. They were almost starved and were ravaged by scurvy. Their diet was reduced to strips of oxhide, softened in seawater, sawdust, and any rats they could catch in their weakened condition.

The people of Guam had never dreamed of such wonders as the ships brought when they anchored in Umatac Bay. The Chamorro sailed out in their swift-flying proas with triangular sails of woven pandanus, bringing fresh fruits and vegetables and other comforts.

64

In return for their kindness many of the Chamorro were murdered by Magellan's men, and it is suspected that the crewmen used the bodies of the murdered natives as an edible cure for their scurvy.

One of Magellan's crew, Gonzalo de Vigo, is said to have jumped ship and lived among the Chamorro for five years before being picked up by Alonso de Salazar's fleet.

After forty years of exploration and discovery, Spain claimed Guam in 1565, and began settlement. The Chamorro were little disturbed by these early contacts with Western civilization until 1668 when a band of Jesuit priests and Spanish soldiers founded the first Christian mission on the island. After 1668 the clash with Spanish priests and soldiers brought change, and after nearly thirty years of bloodshed the Chamorro succumbed to Spanish domination.

Spanish galleons made Guam a regular port of call for two hundred fifty years. Sir Francis Drake and other freebooters and pirates frequently attacked the treasure-laden galleons, with the pirates often hiding out in "Pirates' Cove." The last galleon sailed in 1815, and after that time Guam was more or less isolated, although still under Spanish control.

In 1898 when an American ship sailed in and fired some shots, the Spanish governor had not heard of the Spanish-American War and apologized because he had no ammunition to return the "salutes." In the Treaty of Paris, Spain ceded Guam to the United States.

It is strange that the first violence between the United States and Germany in World War I occurred in far off Guam when the German ship *Cormoran* was scuttled in Apra Harbor, causing the first American gunfire of the war to be fired there.

The Japanese invaded Guam in World War II, and on December 11, 1941, for the first time in the war, the American flag was forced to be lowered on Guam. From that time on, the people of Guam suffered terribly under Japanese occupation. The island was in reality simply one vast prison camp. In July, 1944, six American battleships, nine cruisers and fifty-seven destroyers laid a protecting curtain of fire. Underwater demolition teams worked at night to remove obstacles, and on July 21 the Marines returned. American troops numbered 54,891, and more than a fifth of these became casualties. Over 50,000 Japanese were killed in the battles for Guam, Saipan, and Tinian.

Agaña, capital of Guam, was almost destroyed by the bombardment. Agaña had a population of ten thousand before the war. Its population today is about two thousand.

In 1950, partly as recognition for their loyalty, Guamanians were given United States citizenship. The Organic Act of that year, proclaimed by President Truman, made the island an organized unincorporated territory of the United States, with certain powers of self-government. Supervision was transferred from the navy to the Department of the Interior.

With most of the effects of the war behind them, the people of Guam were dealt another blow, this time by nature. In 1962, typhoon Karen struck the island with a wind velocity of 250 miles (402 kilometers) per hour. The ghastly destruction included almost 90 percent of all the buildings on the island. By some miracle only nine people died, and the people immediately began rebuilding. Most of the new buildings have been designed to withstand the severest winds.

Life on the island is much as it is on the mainland, with television, supermarkets, a highway encircling the island, and a new cable to the mainland. There are public schools, including junior and senior high schools, and parochial schools, including a senior high. The College of Guam was established in 1952 as a two-year college, and is now a four-year accredited institution.

This new "paradise" is different from the old, but apparently the handsome men and beautiful women of Guam have few regrets. They are proud that their beautiful island is known as the "showcase of American democracy in the Far East."

ENCHANTMENT OF GUAM

For the visitor hiking through the lush foliage of Guam, the island offers many pleasures. He may come upon a waterfall such as beautiful Talofofo Falls, or a hidden cave; a small deer may dash off, startled, or a large lizard may shuffle away. The visitor may recognize the rare yoga tree that grows only in the Marianas. The oldest leaves turn red while the others remain green; at the same time there are white blossoms and blue berries. The visitor may also identify the enormous breadfruit tree, which has provided food from time immemorial. He is likely to see coconut palm and betel palm, banyans, and giant figs with their great buttressed roots, the legendary home of ancestral spirits. There will be frequent glimpses of the yellow-flowered shower trees and the terrifically hard ifil tree.

On the brilliant beaches, said by some to be the finest in the world, an unbelievable variety of shells may be found. Toward dusk the rare fanihi or fruit bat may be sighted. The pungent roasted flesh of this very large bat is considered locally to be a great food delicacy. All over the island is the brilliance of the flame tree and the shy hidden beauty of the many orchids, among the three hundred fifty varieties of plants on Guam.

Toward evening the visitor may be treated to an awesomely gorgeous sunset.

Agaña, the capital, is a modern town. Most of what remained of it after World War II could not be rebuilt and had to be bulldozed into the sea. Because Gaum is the only United States free port in the Pacific, Agaña is a shoppers' paradise, with merchandise from all over the world, and fascinating shops such as the South Seas Trading Company, specializing in exotic merchandise of the Far East. The modern Catholic cathedral in Agaña was built in 1958. In the heart of the city is the historic plaza.

More primitive and more picturesque are the villages, nestled in the hills and near the seashore along the highway that encircles the island. The old Spanish bell tower at Merizo is the remnant of the oldest construction on the island. There is a fine church at Inarajan. In contrast are the native thatched houses still to be seen in many places, perched on wooden posts like gaily colored boxes, surrounded by a wealth of tropical flowers.

Almost every town and village has its fiesta. Probably the biggest of these is the one at Inarajan, a seaside village of almost two thousand people. On the fifth weekend after Easter is the Fiesta of St.

Two Lovers' Point

Joseph. After the religious procession and ceremonies, there is a feast of feasts—spicy pork and chicken, saffron rice, curries, shrimp and fish, breadfruit and bananas, cakes and sweets, and perhaps even the fruit bat. Entertainment at the fiesta includes cockfighting, carabao races, and a colorful pageant. Another Inarajan festival is the Coconut Fiesta, featuring a coconut husking competition.

Cockfights are popular throughout the island, and there is much betting and general bedlam as the fights progress in mounting excitement. Another popular feature is racing the chunky, amiable, pink-tongued carabao, probably the favorite beast of the island. Boys of Guam love to tend their carabaos and keep them fat and sleek. Visitors have a chance to take a lumbering ride astride the broad back of a carabao. The animals are still used for hauling to some extent.

The many military installations and the large military population from the United States are the principal sources of the island's prosperity. Military personnel and their families find the island a fascinating place for service. They can enjoy sandy beaches, shelling, swimming, snorkeling, scuba diving, hiking, lagoon fishing, searching for lost Spanish treasure in such spots as Pago Bay, balmy weather, and interesting people. Also, they are able to take leaves to many of the relatively nearby exotic ports of the Far East.

Few visitors to Guam will ever forget its hospitable people and the many charms of this far-off corner of the United States, and most visitors heartily agree with the people of the island who proudly and frequently say, ''Guam is good.''

Right: School in the outer islands. Below: Trade-sailing canoes on the island of Yap in the Caroline Islands.

Micronesia

If some giant hand could lift up the forty-eight mainland United States and put them down gently in the Pacific Ocean, they would only just cover the vast area of about 3,000,000 square miles (7,769,960 square kilometers) of water in which the 2,141 Micronesian islands lie like so many tiny specks.

In this enormous expanse of water, the total land area of those 2,141 islands is only 717 square miles (1,857 square kilometers) — less than half the size of Long Island. They stretch from east to west across 2,700 miles (4,345 kilometers) of the Pacific from north to south for 1,300 miles (2,092 kilometers). Only 96 of the 2,141 islands are regularly inhabited.

There are three major archipelagoes in Micronesia. These island groups are the Carolines, including the Palau Islands and Yap Island; the Marshall Islands; and the Marianas. Although Guam is one of the Marianas, it is, of course, not included with the rest of the Marianas, since Guam is United States territory.

Westernmost of the Micronesian islands is Tobi in the Carolines, at 130° east longitude. Its nearest neighbors are the islands of Indonesia. Easternmost is Mili Atoll in the Marshalls, at 172° east longitude. Mili is about 2000 miles (3,219 kilometers) from the nearest point in Hawaii. Most southerly island is Kapingamarangi in the Carolines, just 1° north of the equator, and the northernmost is Farallon de Pajaros in the Marianas, 20° north latitude.

Between 1947 and 1981 Micronesia was known as the Trust Territory of the Pacific Islands. Under a United Nations mandate, the tiny islands were governed by the United States. Most of the islands are now independent.

The islands of Micronesia are of two types. Low coral atolls only a few feet above the sea level were built up mainly by action of the tiny coral creatures. Others were created by the sharp uprisings of peaks by volcanic action, built up from a vast submarine ridge, some to heights of 2,000 and 3,000 feet (610 and 914 meters). Volcanic action has taken place in recent years on the islands of Pagan in the Marianas. All of the Marshalls and a large part of the Carolines are of the atoll type. Most of the Marianas as well as Yap and the Palau islands are of volcanic origin.

Generally the climate of the islands is moist and tropical. Rainfall is heaviest over the southern half of Micronesia, averaging 120 to 160 inches (305 to 406 centimeters) annually. In the northern section rainfall varies from 60 to 90 inches (152 to 229 centimeters), with pronounced rainy and dry seasons. Some of the islands have extremely dry weather the year round. Fortunately such tropical diseases as malaria, cholera, and yellow fever are not found here.

YESTERDAY AND TODAY

Little is known about the ancient peoples who left such ruins as those as Nanmatol in Ponape and Lele on Kusaie. In 1963 a team of scientists from the Smithsonian Institution conducted research at Nanmatol to study the great prehistoric structures built of log-shaped stones of basalt, placed one above the other as if in a fence or fortress.

It is believed that most of the ancestors of the present native population reached the islands from the Malaysian area after hazardous journeys across open seas. The earliest European explorers found brown-skinned people of medium height, with black hair, low voices, friendly, kind, and generous, and notable for their ability to navigate over tractless wastes of sea in their small sail boats. Most of them traced their inheritance through the mother's side in the matrilineal manner. Most of the present-day population are classified as "Micronesian," although the people of Kapingamarangi and Nukuoro are Polynesian.

Although Ferdinand Magellan passed hundreds of the Micronesian Islands, he actually found only Guam. Later, other Spanish explorers became familiar with the islands around Guam, naming them in honor of Queen Maria Anna of Spain. In 1526 Portuguese discoverers found Yap and Ulithi, and later Spanish voyagers, sighting these and many other islands in the central and southwestern area, named the archipelago Carolina for Charles II of Spain. The Marshalls were discovered by the Spanish in 1529, but named for Engish Captain Marshall who explored them in 1788.

In 1668 a party of Jesuit priests with a small soldier guard established missions on Rota, Tinian, Saipan, and other islands to the north. Only in the late 1800s did Spain extend its rule to include the Carolines and Marshalls.

After the Spanish-American War, Spain withdrew, and in 1899 sold Germany all her remaining Micronesian claims. In 1914 after World War I had begun, Japan took control of the German islands. After the war Japan was given a League of Nations mandate to manage them.

As the American troops began to take the offensive in World War II, names of many of the islands of Micronesia became world famous. Kwajalein in the Marshalls, Saipan and Tinian in the Marianas, and Peleliu in the Carolines were bitterly fought over. Finally they became known as stepping stones in the long hard road back to American mastery of the Pacific. The battle for Peleliu was the heaviest, but the war had a devastating effect on the people of most of the other islands, too.

From 1944 to 1947 Micronesia was administered by a military government. In 1947 President Truman approved the terms under which the United States took over administration of the islands under a trust agreement with the Security Council of the United Nations, which was in line with the trusteeship system established by the United Nations charter. The United States had full powers of administration, legislation, and jurisdiction in this trust territory, reporting to the United Nations regularly on the progress of the trusteeship.

In 1952 a large area around Eniwetok was cleared of ships and people. On November 1, the familiar mushroom cloud of an atomic explosion blasted menacingly into the air above the atoll, but this one was different. This test marked the first full-scale explosion of the much more powerful thermonuclear weapon—the so-called hydrogen bomb. Bikini Atoll also made world headlines as an atomic test center as well as giving its name to a brief bathing suit.

Among the most important events have been the serious typhoons in the late 1950s and the early 1960s, including disastrous typhoon Olive on Saipan in 1963.

THE GOVERNMENT

In 1975, the inhabitants of the Northern Mariana Islands, which include Saipan and Tinian, important World War II bomber bases, voted to become an independent Commonwealth of the United States, much like Puerto Rico. Since April of 1976, these islands have had separate executive and legislative status.

In October 1981, Micronesian leaders met with representatives of the United States on the Hawaiian Island of Maui to finalize years of talks leading to the final independence of most of the islands.

On the basis of these meetings, the Federated States of Micronesia were given the right of self-government. Implementation of the Marshall Islands agreement has been complicated by residents' demand for compensation for nuclear test damages.

THE PEOPLE AND THEIR PROGRESS

The principal aim of the United States government in exercising its trusteeship in Micronesia was to improve the conditions and prospects of the people of the islands. Although nine different major languages are spoken in the area, Micronesians have adopted English as the language in their schools. During the time of the American trusteeship, the U.S. helped to set up an extensive educational system.

But there have been recent problems between the United States and the newly independent islands. Some Micronesians have pro-

74

tested against the continued U.S. military involvement in the Pacific. Also, many residents resent the atomic and hydrogen bomb tests conducted by the United States, during which several islands were blasted away entirely and others left dangerously radioactive for generations. A number of multi-million dollar lawsuits against the U.S. government have been made seeking compensation for damages caused by nuclear testing. In 1983 the United States agreed to a $150 million settlement to the Marshall Islands.

The Micronesians now are taking their own steps to improve their economies. Natives are copying and improving traditional arts and handicrafts to an ever increasing extent. There is a Handicraft and Woodworkers Guild on Palau. Several handicraft shops have now been set up. Some handicrafts are sold to tourists and export companies.

However, the economy at present depends mainly on the coconut palm. From its nut, *copra* (the dried meat of the coconut) is made for export. A strong effort is being carried out to increase cocoa production, and 2 million cocoa seedling trees have been planted. Livestock growing is also being encouraged. Forest lands in the islands total a surprising 80,000 acres (32,375 hectares), including 19,360 acres (7,835 hectares) of valuable mangrove trees. Citrus trees are being introduced where they will grow. The principal exports in addition to copra are scrap metal, handicraft, shells, vegetables, and seafoods.

There are few industries, but in 1964 the VanCamp Company from the United States opened a fish processing plant on Palau, the first outside industry established in the islands since World War II.

Travel over the vast distances is a major problem, but more ships are coming into use, and inter-island air travel is expanding. Many of the islands now have roads such as the 18-mile (29-kilometer) road recently constructed by the people of Arno Atoll. Each district has a broadcasting station, and the use of transistor radios is becoming increasingly popular.

The aerial tramway over the bay in American Samoa.

American Samoa

THE ISLANDS

American Samoa is the most southerly of all lands under United States control. It consists of six small islands; the largest is Tutuila, 18 miles (29 kilometers) long and 6 miles (8 kilometers) wide at the widest point. On Tutuila is the magnificent harbor of Pago Pago (pronounced Pango Pango), where ships are sheltered in the crater of an extinct volcano. The volcanic tops of the islands rise to a maximum height of 3,056 feet (931 meters) on Mt. Lata on Tau Island, second largest of the group. Although 250 miles (402 kilometers) away, Swains Island is administered in the American Samoas.

The climate of the islands is tropical but pleasant. The average rainfall is 200 inches (5.8 meters). Since Samoa is south of the equator, the coolest months are May to November, when the moderate southeast trade winds blow.

Dutch explorer Jacob Roggeveen discovered the Samoan Islands in 1722. Captain John Wilkes of the United States explored there in 1842, and the United States established a naval base in the islands in 1872. Great Britain, Germany, and the United States disputed ownership, and it appeared that a battle would take place in 1889, but the conflict was swept away by a typhoon. Three German and three United States ships were either wrecked or thrown ashore by the terrific winds. The single British ship escaped through the storm.

In 1899 the Samoan Islands were divided into a western group under the control of Germany and an American group under the United States. Western Samoa has been an independent country since 1962. American Samoa is an unorganized unincorporated territory of the United States, administered by the Department of the Interior. The people are American nationals. In 1978 native islander Peter Tali Coleman became the first popularly elected governor. Under the constitution approved in 1960, there is a two-house legislature with limited authority. According to the constitution, ''It shall be the policy of the government of American Samoa to protect persons of Samoan ancestry against alienation of their lands and destruction of the Samoan way of life and language." Land ownership is retained by the Samoan people, and no one of less than 50 percent Samoan blood may purchase real estate, with some few small exceptions.

In 1961 *Reader's Digest* called United States neglect of the islands "shame in the South Seas." Then Governor H. Rex Lee was appointed, and he moved swiftly to help the islanders help themselves.

One of Governor Lee's most notable accomplishments was to set up the first "whole system" educational television programming ever tried anywhere. Realizing the difficulties in training teachers and the problems of consolidating schools from island to island, the Samoan leaders persuaded Congress to provide funds for a broadcasting station and three hundred 23-inch (58-centimeter) television receivers to be installed in the fifty-three public elementary schools scattered throughout the islands. The system is being extended to secondary school work.

Television teaching began on October 5, 1964. Children sit in their local classrooms on the floor in traditional Samoan manner watching their television lessons with rapt attention under the direction of the local teachers. A number of the television teachers have become television "personalities" with devoted fans. After school, the teachers are given a television coaching session on the next day's lesson. Television teaching is already considered to have improved the island's education to a large extent.

There is one public high school in the islands, enrolling over 2,000 students. It is said to rank with many good high schools on the mainland. There is also a private high school.

THE PEOPLE

The people of Samoa have been described as "one of the few remaining societies retaining the major part of their traditional culture." They continue to live much as they always have, in easy harmony with soil and sea. Some consider them to be the only dependent race never to have been "exploited, demeaned, or dispossessed." The majority of the people are still of unmixed blood, clinging to their old ways while accepting those particular Western ways that seem to enhance their traditional life. They have been described as "warm, life-loving people who have found paradise and want to keep it."

Eight children in a family is about average. Families of eighteen are not uncommon. At one time children were often given a name that reminded their parents of something—High Tide, Jeep, Jet, Petty Officer, or Cricket Club. The "extended family" group, all those related in a family, called *aiga,* is the principal unit of Samoan society. Each aiga elects its *matai* (leader or chief) to speak for it. Nowhere is there greater respect for the family. No member of an aiga goes hungry or in need. That would disgrace his family.

The traditional wrap-around garment, the lavalava, is still worn regularly. Many a tattooed tribal or government chief may be seen going about his duties in a lavalava. For meetings of the legislature the men are mostly in lavalavas, but on Sunday there is a spotless white suit coat over the tailored lavalava for church.

Almost since the first missionary in Samoa arrived in 1830 from the London Missionary Society to establish a Samoan church, large numbers of the people have been devout Christians, serious students of the Bible who love to argue intricate points of theology.

However, no matter how serious and industrious they may be, and they are both, underneath they are laughing, happy Polynesians, enjoying themselves as only the Samoans can. They love to sing and dance. The Samoan dance, called *siva,* is different from the Hawaiian. The siva is full of leaping steps and rhythmic clapping. The Samoan language, though, is similar to the Hawaiian, and as in Hawaii, the single girl wears a bloom over her left ear to show she is unmarried.

There is no housing shortage; any able-bodied man can build and thatch the traditional *fale.* The fale is completely open to the passerby, with no walls or doors; it catches every passing breeze. Mats can be let down in case of a blowing rain. Outside grow breadfruit, papaya, and mango trees for food. Hibiscus and other tropical flowers provide plentiful decoration.

Most American Samoans are Polynesians.

"FAUSIA SE SAMOA FOU": BUILDING A NEW SAMOA

In Samoa the soil is "so rich that the fence posts sometimes take root." Coconuts are the principal crop. Dried coconut kernels called copra yield coconut oil. Samoan cocoa ranks among the best in the world, and the acreage of cocoa trees is being increased. Bananas make up the third most important crop. Increasingly large herds of cattle graze on lush grass under the tall coconut trees.

Some of the finest craftwork in the Polynesian tradition is still being produced in American Samoa. Baskets and laufala floor mats are woven from palm leaves. Tapa cloth is pounded from the bark of the paper mulberry tree. To create the bright designs on the tapa cloth, the plain cloth is pressed against inked wood-printing blocks in which traditional designs have been cut. Tapa cloth is still much used for lavalavas, although Samoan women also cherish imported goods.

Samoans are skilled in hollowing out canoes from tree trunks to make small outrigger craft for fishing. Many-oared longboats called *fautasi* are sometimes 40 feet (12 meters) long. Shore fishing is done by hurling huge nets into the sea, in a process requiring great skill.

Chicken of the Sea tuna is now being packed in American Samoa and is presently the largest industry. Star Kist Tuna Company is also operating, and the American Can Company has a plant providing containers for both packers.

The government is pushing a development program to increase Samoan resources and effectiveness in all these fields while still retaining the policy of "Samoa for the Samoans."

ENCHANTMENT OF AMERICAN SAMOA

These islands, which Rupert Brooke called "lovely and lost and half the world away," are still half the world away, but with Pago Pago International Airport, completed in 1964, they are only a jet-hop distant.

Here are beaches of luminous beauty, where black volcanic rock, white coral sand, and green palms combine in dazzling scenes of beauty; mountain and forest, flowing stream and frothing surf, lazy lagoon, all blend into a vision of ageless serenity.

Visitors may still see the boarding house where Somerset Maugham sighted Sadie Thompson. Pago Pago was the setting for his short story *Rain,* made into a movie under the title *Sadie Thompson.* Visitors will also be interested to ride the soaring cable car crossing high above sparkling Pago Pago Bay, creeping up its 5,103-foot (1,555-meter) cable to the lofty top of Mount Alava.

One of the unusual experiences of Samoa and a treat visitors never forget is the delight of its most delicious dish—palusami—a thick cream of coconut, cooked within a fresh taro leaf and served on slices of taro.

Tourism has not been encouraged until recently, but a new hotel and other facilities now make more tourism possible. The new buildings that have been built, such as the eight hundred seat Lee Auditorium, have kept the architectural feeling of the isle. The auditorium was named in honor of Governor H. Rex Lee.

Americans who visit are almost sure to agree with the Samoans who, because they are also Americans, can say as did Talking Chief (Chief Clan Spokesman) Olo, "I doubt if there are any other people like us who literally get the best of two worlds."

81

Part of the circular outer barrier reef around Midway Islands.

Other Pacific Islands

MIDWAY ISLANDS

The Midway group consists of an island and two islets—Easter and Sand islands. The lagoon, surrounded by a coral reef, is crystal clear; the white beaches are said to surpass Waikiki. The islands are 1,150 miles (1,850 kilometers) northwest of Honolulu and are geographically part of the Hawaiians. They are in the geographical center, or midway, of the north Pacific. Their climate is warm and humid, with 92 degrees Fahrenheit (33.3 degrees Celsius) the highest and 54 degrees Fahrenheit (12.2 degrees Celsius) the lowest temperatures ever recorded.

Midway was discovered by United States Captain U.C. Brooks in 1859 and annexed by the United States in 1867. In 1904 the first U.S. garrison arrived there, and Midway began to serve as a relay station for the Pacific cable that year. Pan American World Airways established a base for its planes there in 1935.

After attacking Pearl Harbor, the Japanese planes attacked Midway on the way back, and the first Congressional Medal of Honor winner of the war, George Cannon, was killed in that attack. One of history's pivotal battles was fought there in June, 1942, when United States Navy planes routed a Japanese armada in what has been thought of as the turning point of the war in the Pacific.

Today, military personnel and those servicing the various installations are the only permanent inhabitants, dwelling among the lush vegetable growth of trees, shrubs, flowers, and grasses.

One of Midway's most outstanding features is its bird life, especially the pesky gooney bird. This huge albatross with a wingspread of 6 to 7 feet (1.8 to 2.1 meters) is afraid of nothing. The birds follow people about, clacking their bills and rubbing against their legs. On land they are clumsy clowns. In the air they appear as the spirit of grace. They spend most of their time at sea, returning to land only to nest. The gooneys always return to their ancestral nesting grounds, and remember exactly where their nests are. Those who nested where the runways now are always return there and no means have been found to keep them away. They collide with planes, damaging them severely. Fortunately in over 2,000 collisions there have been no human casualties.

Other interesting Midway birds include flitting canaries, boobies, frigate, bosun, the gentle love tern, and the shearwater, called the moaning bird because of its cry, like a fretful baby. It is estimated there are six hundred thousand sooty terns, five hundred thousand shearwater, and fifty thousand gooney birds on Midway.

WAKE ISLAND

Wake consists of a coral atoll and three islets connected by a causeway, lying roughly midway between Hawaii and Guam. The United States claimed it formally in 1900, but it was deserted until 1935 when Pan American Airways built a forty-five-room hotel there as a stopover on its transpacific runs. They found the island overrun with Philippine rats, birds, and hermit crabs. The island serves as a refueling stop for some airplanes.

JOHNSTON ATOLL AND SAND ISLAND

Johnston Atoll and its satellite, Sand Island, lie 715 miles (1,151 kilometers) southwest of Honolulu. In 1858 both the United States and the Kingdom of Hawaii annexed it. Today, however, it is not administered as part of Hawaii. For years it was a bird reservation and then became a U.S. naval station.

KINGMAN REEF

This islet, less than half a mile square (1.3 square kilometers), lies about 1,000 miles (1,609 kilometers) southeast of Johnston. It was discovered in 1874 by Americans and annexed by the United States in 1922.

PALMYRA

The atoll of Palmyra is made up of about fifty islets, located about 960 miles (1,545 kilometers) south-southwest of Honolulu. It had been claimed by the Kingdom of Hawaii, and in 1912 the United States formally annexed it. When Hawaii became a state, Palmyra was excluded from it. Palmyra was discovered in 1802 by Captain Sawle of the American ship *Palmyra*. Today it has an emergency landing strip for planes and is privately owned. The islands are covered with dense foliage, including coconut and the balsa-like pisonia grandis, which grows 100 feet (30 meters) high. The highest elevation in the Palmyra group is 30 feet (9 meters).

HOWLAND, BAKER, AND JARVIS

Although these three islands are widely separated, they are strikingly similar in appearance and history. Howland and Baker lie a few miles to the north of the equator and Jarvis to the south. Jarvis lies about 1,100 miles (1,770 kilometers) east of the other two, which are quite close together.

All three were originally claimed in 1857 by the United States and formally proclaimed as United States territory in 1935-36, when they were placed under the Department of Interior. In 1936 the department established a few American colonists who were evacuated in 1942, and there have been no inhabitants since.

Only a little grass and brushwood grow on Howland, but typical Pacific birds are abundant. Baker has less bird life because of the bird-eating Norway rat. Jarvis is rich in guano, and fish in large numbers are found in pools in the reef.

CANTON, ENDERBURY, AND OTHER DISPUTED ISLANDS

Twenty-five islands in an area of the Pacific about the size of the Caribbean are claimed by the United States. Claim to eighteen of these is disputed by the United Kingdom. New Zealand claims ownership of the other seven.

The largest of the disputed territories is Canton Island in the Phoenix Islands. It consists of a thin strip of coral land almost completely encircling a large clear lagoon 8 miles (13 kilometers) long and 4 miles (6 kilometers) wide. The width of the land area varies from 60 to 600 yards (55 to 550 meters), and it never rises more than 20 feet (6 meters).

Its discovery date is not known; Canton is not on maps of 1791 but was mentioned in a United States Navy report of 1828. It takes its name from the New Bedford whaling ship *Canton,* which was wrecked there in March, 1854. The shipwrecked men made it to the island in the ship's small boats, but when the supplies began to give out, they started across the open seas. After 45 days of terrible hardship they reached Tinian, but the Spanish commander would not let them stay, so they went on for four more days until reaching Guam. No lives were lost, but they suffered greatly from hunger and thirst during their remarkable journey.

An American group worked the guano of Enderbury Island in 1858, and Canton was worked for this fertilizer by British companies during the last half of the 1800s.

Both the United Kingdom and the United States claim Canton, Enderbury, and sixteen other islands in the region. These include the other Phoenix islands, the Line Islands, and Ellice Islands. The best known of the islands is Christmas Island in the Line group.

British and American groups sent scientific expeditions to Canton in 1936, and both sides planted their own flags. In 1938, President Franklin D. Roosevelt placed Canton and Enderbury under the Department of the Interior. In 1939, the two nations agreed to occupy the disputed islands jointly until rights to them were established at a later date.

Title to seven other nearby islands is disputed between the United States and New Zealand. These are the D. Tokelau or Union Islands and the E. Northern Cook Islands. All except five of the twenty-five disputed islands have some inhabitants.

Bird population of the islands is picturesque. Most startling is the

86

man-o'-war bird (frigate bird) with its brilliant red inflated throat sac, and 7-foot (2-meter) wingspread, one of the world's best fliers. The long scarlet tail feather of the red-tailed tropic or boatswains bird is much prized.

There are many fish, a few lizards, butterflies, and grasshoppers, and the islands are overrun with hermit crabs, crawling about inside their borrowed shells.

Vegetation is sparse, but the native scaevola tree grows about 15 feet (4.5 meters) high.

Handy Reference Section

Instant Facts

Commonwealth of Puerto Rico

Became a commonwealth July 25, 1952
Capital—San Juan, settled 1508
Commonwealth official anthem—"La Borinqueñe," music by Felix Astol y Artés
Flag—Three red and two white horizontal stripes, with a blue triangle at the mast
    bearing one white star
Area—3,435 square miles (8,897 square kilometers)
Greatest length (north to south)—about 36 miles (58 kilometers)
Greatest width (east to west)—about 100 miles (161 kilometers)
Highest point—4,389 feet (1,338 meters), Cerro de Punta
Lowest point—Sea level
Population—3,187,570 (1980 census)
Population density—928 persons per square mile (358 persons per kilometer),
    1980 census

Principal cities—		
San Juan	432,973	(1980 census)
Bayamón	195,965	
Ponce	188,219	
Carolina	165,207	
Mayaqüez	95,886	
Arecibo	86,660	
Guaynabo	80,857	

Virgin Islands of the United States

Accession proclaimed March 21, 1917
Capital—Charlotte Amalie, on St. Thomas since 1917
Official flower—Yellow elder or yellow cedar
Official bird—Yellow breast
Official song—"Virgin Islands March"
Land area—128 square miles (332 square kilometers)
  St. Croix—82 square miles (212 square kilometers)
  St. Thomas—27 square miles (70 square kilometers)
  St. John—19 square miles (49 square kilometers)
Highest point—1,556 feet (474 meters), Crown Mountain on St. Thomas
Lowest point—Sea level
Population—95,591 (1980 census)

Principal cities—		
Charlotte Amalie	11,756	(all 1980 census)
Christiansted	2,856	

Guam

Ceded by Spain, December 10, 1898
Became a United States Territory, August 1, 1950
Capital—Agaña
Nickname—Pearl of the Pacific
Official flower—Bougainvillea *(Putitai nobio)*
Official bird—Fruit dove
Official animal—Iguana
Official stone—Latte
Official song—"Stand Ye Guamanians"
Area—212 square miles (549 square kilometers)
Greatest length (north to south)—30 miles (48 kilometers)
Greatest width (east to west)—8.5 miles (13.7 kilometers)
Population—105,979 (1980 census)
Principal cities—Tamuning   8,862 (all 1980 census)
                Yigo   3,392
                Agana Heights 2,970
                Dededo   2,524
                Mongmong   2,058

Micronesia

Most islands under U.S. from July 1947 to October 1981
Administrative center—Kolonia, Ponale
North Marianas will become a U.S. commonwealth
Balance of territory scheduled for independence
Area—717 square miles (1,857 square kilometers) of land
Population—116,974 (1980 estimate)
Population, Saipan—14,335 (1976 estimate)
Major islands—Caroline Islands, Marshall Islands, and Mariana Islands (except
                Guam)

American Samoa

Territorial progression — 1899-1900 and 1904
Capital — Pago Pago, population 3,075 (1980 census)
Motto — *Samoa Muamua Le Atua* (In Samoa, God is First)
Official flower — Paogo *(Ula-fala)*
Official tree — Moso'oi
Official plant — Ava
Official song — "Amerika Samoa"
Area — 76 square miles (197 square kilometers)
Highest point — 3,056 feet (931 meters), Mt. Lata, Tau Island
Population — 32,297 (1980 census)

LISTING OF ISLANDS WITHIN CERTAIN GROUPS

Principal Caroline Islands and atolls: Angaur, Babelthuap, Eauripik, Fais, Faraulep, Gaferut, Hall, Helen, Ifalik, Kapingamarangi, Kusaie, Merir, Mortlock, Namonuito, Ngatik, Ngulu, Nukuoro, Oroluk, Palau, Peleliu, Pigailoe, Pingelap, Ponape, Pulap, Pulo Anna, Pulusuk, Puluwat, Satawal, Senyavin, Sonsorol, Tobi, Truk, Ulithi, Woleai, Yap

Principal Mariana Islands and atolls (formerly Ladron Islands): Agrihan, Aguijan, Alamagan, Anatahan, Asuncion, Guguan, Maug, Medinilla, Pagan, Farallon de Pajaros, Rota, Saipan, Sarigan, Tinian

Principal Marshall Islands and atolls: Ralik and Ratak chains and individual islands: Ailinglapalap, Arno, Bikini, Ebon, Eniwetok, Jaluit, Kili, Kwajalein, Majuro, Maloelap, Mili, Namorik, Rongelap, Taongi, Ujelang, Utirik, Wotje

Line Islands: Caroline Atoll, Christmas Island, Flint Island, Malden Island, Starbuck Island, Vostok Island

Ellice Islands: Funafuti Atoll, Nukufetau Atoll, Nukulailai Atoll (Nukulaelae), Nurakita

Phoenix Islands: Birnie Atoll, Gardner Atoll, Hull Atoll, McKean Atoll, Sydney Atoll, Phoenix Atoll, Canton, Enderbury

D.Tokelau (or Union) Islands: Atafu Atoll, Fafaofu Atoll, Nukunono Atoll

E. Northern Cook Islands: Danger Atoll, Manahiki Atoll, Rakahanga Atoll, Penrhyn Atoll

OUTLYING AREA ASSOCIATED WITH THE UNITED STATES
FACTS AND COMPARISONS

CARIBBEAN AREAS

Name	Capital	Population	U.S. Dept. Responsible	Government, type or arrangement
Puerto Rico	San Juan	3,187,570	none	Commonwealth
Virgin Islands of the United States	Charlotte Amalie	95,591	Interior	Organized, uninc. ter.
Panama Canal			none	Incorporated into Panama in 1979
Navassa	none	0	Coast Guard	Uninc. pos.

PACIFIC ISLANDS

Name	Capital	Population	U.S. Dept. Responsible	Government, type or arrangement
Guam	Agaña	105,979	Interior	Organized uninc. ter.
Northern Marianas	Garapan, Saipan	16,758	Interior, until 1981	Commonwealth, 1981
Micronesia	Kolonia, Ponape	116,662	Interior	Scheduled for independence
American Samoa	Pago Pago	32,297	Interior	Unorganized uninc. ter.
Midway	none	2,256	Navy	Uninc. pos.
Wake	none	300	Interior	Possession
Johnston and Sand	none	1,007	Air Force	Uninc. pos.
Palmyra	none	1	Interior	Uninc. pos.
Kingman Reef	none	0	Navy	Uninc. pos.
Howland, Baker, and Jarvis	none	0	Interior	Possessions
Canton and Enderbury	none	0	Interior	Controlled jointly by Britain and U.S. by treaty until 1989
Other disputed Islands	none		State	Status Quo

Note: Incorporated territory refers to an area which Congress has "incorporated" into the United States by making the Constitution apply to it. Unincorporated territory or possession is any territory to which the Constitution has not been expressly and fully extended. The U.S. government retains rights to military bases and the canal within the former Panama Canal Zone.

Rank in Area

1 Puerto Rico . . . . 3,435 square miles
(8,897 square kilometers)
2 Micronesia . . . . 717 square miles
(1,857 square kilometers)
3 Guam . . . . 212 square miles
(549 square kilometers)
4 Virgin Islands . . . . 128 square miles
(332 square kilometers)
5 American Samoa . . . . 76 square miles
(197 square kilometers)

Rank in Population

1 Puerto Rico 3,187,570
(1980 census)
2 Micronesia 116,662
(1980 estimate)
3 Guam 105,979
(1980 census)
4 Virgin Islands 95,591
(1980 census)
5 American Samoa 32,297
(1980 census)

Index

94

PICTURE CREDITS

ABOUT THE AUTHOR

With the publication of his first book for school use when he was twenty, **Allan Carpenter** began a career as an author that has spanned more than 135 books. After teaching in the public schools of Des Moines, Mr. Carpenter began his career as an educational publisher at the age of twenty-one when he founded the magazine *Teachers Digest*. In the field of educational periodicals, he was responsible for many innovations. During his many years in publishing, he has perfected a highly organized approach to handling large volumes of factual material: after extensive traveling and having collected all possible materials, he systematically reviews and organizes everything. From his apartment high in Chicago's John Hancock Building, Allan recalls, "My collection and assimilation of materials on the states and countries began before the publication of my first book." Allan is the founder of Carpenter Publishing House and of Infordata International, Inc., publishers of *Issues in Education* and *Index to U. S. Government Periodicals*. When he is not writing or traveling, his principal avocation is music. He has been the principal bassist of many symphonies, and he managed the country's leading non-professional symphony for twenty-five years.